Lift Application Development Cookbook

Over 50 practical recipes to build web applications using Lift, the most secure web framework available

Gilberto T. Garcia Jr.

[PACKT] PUBLISHING

BIRMINGHAM - MUMBAI

Lift Application Development Cookbook

First published: September 2013

Production Reference: 1190913

Published by Packt Publishing Ltd.
Livery Place
35 Livery Street
Birmingham B3 2PB, UK.

ISBN 978-1-84951-588-7

www.packtpub.com

Cover Image by Suresh Mogre (suresh.mogre.99@gmail.com)

Credits

Author

Gilberto T. Garcia Jr.

Reviewers

Diego Medina

Peter Petersson (karma4u101)

Peter Robinett

Paulo Suzart

Acquisition Editor

Vinay Argekar

Lead Technical Editor

Azharuddin Sheikh

Technical Editors

Jalasha D'costa

Akashdeep Kundu

Proshonjit Mitra

Shiny Poojary

Copy Editors

Brandt D'Mello

Mradula Hegde

Gladson Monteiro

Project Coordinator

Angel Jathanna

Proofreaders

Simran Bhogal

Ameesha Green

Indexer

Rekha Nair

Graphics

Abhinash Sahu

Production Coordinator

Nilesh R. Mohite

Cover Work

Nilesh R. Mohite

About the Author

Gilberto T. Garcia Jr. has a Bachelor's degree in Philosophy from USP, and has been working with Internet-related technologies since 1999. He had worked with different programming languages in several projects with different sizes and complexities.

As a person who enjoys learning new things, he started to study and work with Scala and Lift in 2010.

I want to thank my wife, Lavinia, for all the love and encouragement to write this book, and for her support and patience during the writing process. I also want to thank my family and friends.

Thanks to David Pollak for creating Lift, and thanks to the Lift committers and everyone who makes the Lift community such a nice place to be around.

About the Reviewers

Diego Medina lives on the mountains of North Carolina with his wife, daughter, and their three cats. He has been a developer for the past 12 years, and his focus has been on web development and more specifically, web security.

He is a proud Lift committer and a very active member of the Lift community, answering questions on the mailing list as well as writing articles on his personal blog.

Peter Petersson lives in the south of Sweden with his wife and one-year-old boy.

He has been a developer for 18 years. He started his developer career at Ericsson Software Technology mostly using C++, but at the time Java was emerging, he soon jumped onto that bandwagon. He has been a co-owner in a tour operator information system company and is currently a system developer and consultant at Avalon Innovation.

He started looking at Scala and functional programing at the beginning of 2011, about the same time he found Lift to be an awesome web framework. He is a proud Lift committer and creator of the Lift FoBo, Front End Toolkit Module, as well as the jQuery module.

Peter Robinett is a web and mobile developer based in Amsterdam. He is passionate about Scala and is a committer to the Lift project. He works under the name Bubble Foundry, and blogs occasionally at `www.bubblefoundry.com`.

Paulo Suzart worked in different types of companies in the last 10 years, from e-commerce to insurance, as a Java programmer and lately as an SOA specialist. He currently runs a digital media startup as CTO.

He truly believes that startups are open fields for new technologies and functional programming languages, such as Scala and Clojure.

www.PacktPub.com

Support files, eBooks, discount offers and more

You might want to visit www.PacktPub.com for support files and downloads related to your book.

Did you know that Packt offers eBook versions of every book published, with PDF and ePub files available? You can upgrade to the eBook version at www.PacktPub.com and as a print book customer, you are entitled to a discount on the eBook copy. Get in touch with us at service@packtpub.com for more details.

At www.PacktPub.com, you can also read a collection of free technical articles, sign up for a range of free newsletters and receive exclusive discounts and offers on Packt books and eBooks.

http://PacktLib.PacktPub.com

Do you need instant solutions to your IT questions? PacktLib is Packt's online digital book library. Here, you can access, read and search across Packt's entire library of books.

Why Subscribe?

- ▸ Fully searchable across every book published by Packt
- ▸ Copy and paste, print and bookmark content
- ▸ On demand and accessible via web browser

Free Access for Packt account holders

If you have an account with Packt at www.PacktPub.com, you can use this to access PacktLib today and view nine entirely free books. Simply use your login credentials for immediate access.

Table of Contents

Preface

Lift is a web framework built in Scala. Its main goal is to be a secure framework that helps developers to build scalable web applications in a concise and maintainable way.

There are six things—according to the official website, `http://liftweb.net/`—that makes Lift different from any other web framework available today:

- **Secure**: Lift apps are resistant to common vulnerabilities, including many of the OWASP Top 10 projects
- **Developer-centric**: Lift apps are fast to build, concise, and easy to maintain
- **Designer-friendly**: Lift apps can be developed in a totally designer-friendly way
- **Scalable**: Lift has a number of high-performance apps, and they scale in the real world to handle insane traffic levels
- **Modular**: Lift apps can benefit from easy-to-integrate, pre-built modules
- **Interactive like a desktop app**: Lift's Comet support is unparalleled, and Lift's Ajax support is super easy and very secure

The goal of this book is to introduce you to the basics of Lift, and teach you everything that you need to know to build applications using Lift.

By providing you with hands-on examples, we hope that you find this book useful as your first introduction to Lift, and also as a reference guide when building your own web applications.

What this book covers

Chapter 1, *Getting Started with Lift Basics*, covers the basics of Lift which include how to start a new application using build tools such as SBT and Maven. It also explains how to define the application structure using SiteMap object and how to use the Mailer object to send e-mails.

Chapter 2, *Working with HTML*, introduces the reader to CSS selectors and shows how to use them to transform the HTML that will be rendered in the browser. It also covers how to test snippets, how to generate a JavaScript code from the server, and how to invoke server-side functions using JavaScript. It also explains how to localize templates.

Chapter 3, Working with Forms, covers the different ways the reader can work with forms, such as how to create a single page form and a wizard-like form. It also explains how to submit forms using Ajax and how to wire form fields.

Chapter 4, Working with REST, introduces Lift's `RestHelper` object and how to use it to create a REST API. It also explains how to test the REST API, how to upload files, and how to create an RSS feed.

Chapter 5, Working with Databases, explains how to use Mapper to integrate the application with a database. It also covers the basics of ORM mapping and how to use an in-memory database to test an application that uses Mapper.

Chapter 6, Working with Record, explains how to integrate a Lift application with a database using Record and Squeryl. It also covers how to test an application that uses Record and Squeryl using an in-memory database.

Chapter 7, Working with MongoDB, covers the integration of a Lift application with MongoDB, how to use Record to create such an integration, and explains how to query MongoDB using Rogue.

Chapter 8, Integrating Lift with Social Media, explains how to use social login to authenticate users and how to get their data from their Facebook, Gmail, Twitter, or LinkedIn accounts.

What you need for this book

To be able to follow the recipes, you will need to have Java 7 installed on your computer.

Who this book is for

This book is for developers who want to learn how to develop web applications using the Lift framework. However, we assume that the reader at least knows the basics of Scala, HTML, and JavaScript.

Conventions

In this book, you will find a number of styles of text that distinguish between different kinds of information. Here are some examples of these styles, and an explanation of their meaning.

Code words in text, database table names, folder names, filenames, file extensions, pathnames, dummy URLs, user input, and Twitter handles are shown as follows: "The bigger difference lies in the snippet code. You can see that after getting the user data, we've invoked a method called `fetchUserData` and used its result to change the contents of a `li` tag."

A block of code is set as follows:

```
import code.lib.googleSession
import net.liftweb.util.BindHelpers._
import net.liftweb.common.Full

object GmailData {
  def render = {
    googleSession.get match {
      case Full(email) => ".email" #> email
      case _ =>  "*" #> "Not authorized"
    }
  }
}
```

When we wish to draw your attention to a particular part of a code block, the relevant lines or items are set in bold:

```
          <pubDate> {longDate(Calendar.getInstance().getTimeInMillis)}
</pubDate>
          {ClientCache.clients.flatMap {
          c =>
            <item>
              <title>Client: {c.id}</title>
              <description>Name: {c.name} - E-mail:
{c.email}</description>
```

Any command-line input or output is written as follows:

```
scala> val transformSpanContent = "span *" #> "Some Text"
```

New terms and **important words** are shown in bold. Words that you see on the screen, in menus or dialog boxes for example, appear in the text like this: "If you select a name in the combobox and click on the **Delete Selected** button, you'll see an alert saying that the name you selected was deleted."

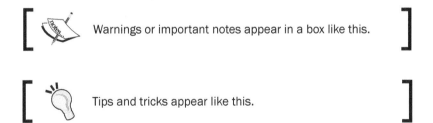

Warnings or important notes appear in a box like this.

Tips and tricks appear like this.

Reader feedback

Feedback from our readers is always welcome. Let us know what you think about this book—what you liked or may have disliked. Reader feedback is important for us to develop titles that you really get the most out of.

To send us general feedback, simply send an e-mail to feedback@packtpub.com, and mention the book title via the subject of your message.

If there is a topic that you have expertise in and you are interested in either writing or contributing to a book, see our author guide on www.packtpub.com/authors.

Customer support

Now that you are the proud owner of a Packt book, we have a number of things to help you to get the most from your purchase.

Downloading the example code

You can download the example code files for all Packt books you have purchased from your account at http://www.packtpub.com. If you purchased this book elsewhere, you can visit http://www.packtpub.com/support and register to have the files e-mailed directly to you.

Errata

Although we have taken every care to ensure the accuracy of our content, mistakes do happen. If you find a mistake in one of our books—maybe a mistake in the text or the code—we would be grateful if you would report this to us. By doing so, you can save other readers from frustration and help us improve subsequent versions of this book. If you find any errata, please report them by visiting http://www.packtpub.com/submit-errata, selecting your book, clicking on the **errata submission form** link, and entering the details of your errata. Once your errata are verified, your submission will be accepted and the errata will be uploaded on our website, or added to any list of existing errata, under the Errata section of that title. Any existing errata can be viewed by selecting your title from http://www.packtpub.com/support.

Piracy

Piracy of copyright material on the Internet is an ongoing problem across all media. At Packt, we take the protection of our copyright and licenses very seriously. If you come across any illegal copies of our works, in any form, on the Internet, please provide us with the location address or website name immediately so that we can pursue a remedy.

Please contact us at copyright@packtpub.com with a link to the suspected pirated material.

We appreciate your help in protecting our authors, and our ability to bring you valuable content.

Questions

You can contact us at questions@packtpub.com if you are having a problem with any aspect of the book, and we will do our best to address it.

1
Getting Started with Lift Basics

In this chapter, we will learn about:

- ▶ Creating a Lift application using SBT
- ▶ Creating a Lift application using Maven
- ▶ Defining a SiteMap
- ▶ Logging using logback
- ▶ Sending e-mails using Gmail's SMTP server

Introduction

In this chapter, we will learn how to install Lift, which is a very secure web framework written in Scala; how to configure the basics of a Lift application such as how to define the SiteMap which is a comprehensive representation of the pages of a Lift application; and how to configure a log engine. We will also learn how to create an application using **Simple Build Tool** (**SBT**) or Maven.

Creating a Lift application using SBT

SBT is a build tool for Scala and Java projects. The idea of using a build tool such as SBT is to make it easier to manage all of the project dependencies. Also, it helps to ensure that the application generated by the build process is always the same. This means that it doesn't matter whether the application is built on my computer or yours, the end result will be the same.

The easiest way to start with Lift and SBT is by downloading them from the official website. There, you can find a list of `tar.gz` and `.zip` files containing everything you need to start using Lift.

Getting ready

Scala, and in turn, the Lift development requires a JVM and because of this, you'll need to install Java 7 on your computer. However, you can skip this step if you already have it installed. If not then go to `http://java.com` and click on the **Free Java Download** button. Then, download and install the JDK appropriate for your OS.

How to do it...

Carry out the following steps:

1. First of all, to install and run Lift on Windows, you will need to download the `Lift 2.5` ZIP file, which is the latest stable release, from `http://liftweb.net/download`.

2. After the download is complete, open Windows Explorer and extract the contents from the file.

3. Then, go to `scala_210/ift_basic`, double click on the `sbt.bat` file to run SBT, and wait until SBT finishes downloading the required libraries. This process can take a while depending on the speed of your internet connection.

   When the download part is completed, you will get the SBT prompt that can be recognized by the > character.

4. After getting into the SBT prompt, type the following command to start the basic Lift application:

   ```
   > container:start
   ```

5. At this point, we have a running Lift application. So, open up your favorite browser and go to `http://localhost:8080`. Then you should see a welcome window similar to the following screenshot:

6. To exit SBT, you just need to type the following command in the SBT prompt:

   ```
   > exit
   ```

How it works...

The ZIP file contains some examples of Lift applications such as a blank application that you can use to start your application from scratch. It also contains a basic Lift application that contains **Blueprint CSS** and ready-to-use **Mapper models,** which you can use as the start point when building your own application.

The `lift_basic` folder contains a working Lift application. This means that you have SBT and a configured, ready-to-use project in it.

When we ran SBT, it started to download all the required libraries that the application needs (these dependencies are defined in the `build.sbt` file). Once this step is done, we can start the application.

After downloading the required libraries, we ran the `container:start` command provided by the sbt-web-plugin that deploys the Lift application into an embedded Jetty server.

You can see that inside the `lift_basic` application, there is a folder called `project` which contains a file called `project.sbt`. In that file, you will see that it defines three plugins for SBT. The first defined plugin is the XSBT plugin. After the XSBT plugin, there is the sbt-idea plugin and the sbteclipse plugin. The former is to enable SBT to be integrated with IntelliJ IDEA, and the latter enables SBT to be integrated with Scala IDE. Another thing to notice in the `plugins.sbt` file is that it matches the version of SBT to select the correct version of the sbt-web-plugin.

There's more...

To install and run Lift on Linux or Mac, perform the following steps:

1. Download the `Lift 2.5 ZIP` or the `tar.gz` file from `http://liftweb.net/download`.

2. Once you've got the file, open a shell tool and expand it.

3. Then, go to `scala_210/lift_basic`, and start SBT by running the following command:

   `./sbt`

4. You can then continue from step 4 of the *How to do it...* section.

See also

▶ You can read the `README.md` file and explore each sample application folder to learn more about what is bundled within Lift's ZIP file

▶ You can find more about the sbt-web-plugin at the following URL:
`https://github.com/JamesEarlDouglas/xsbt-web-plugin`

- ▶ Please navigate to `https://github.com/mpeltonen/sbt-idea` to get to know more about the SBT plugin for IntelliJ IDEA
- ▶ Please navigate to `https://github.com/typesafehub/sbteclipse` to learn more about the SBT plugin for ScalaIDE/Eclipse
- ▶ To find more about SBT, please go to `http://www.scala-sbt.org/`

Creating a Lift application using Maven

In the previous recipe, we learned how to use SBT to create and run a Lift application. Now I will show you how to set up and run a Lift application using Maven, which is another build tool.

Getting ready

If you don't have Maven installed and configured on your computer, go to `http://maven.apache.org/download.cgi`, download Maven 3.1.0, and follow the installation instructions.

How to do it...

We will use a Maven archetype that will create a ready-to-use Lift application for us.

1. Open a cmd window and run the following command:

```
mvn archetype:generate ^
  -DarchetypeGroupId=net.liftweb ^
  -DarchetypeArtifactId=lift-archetype-basic_2.9.1 ^
  -DarchetypeVersion=2.5 ^
  -DarchetypeRepository=https://oss.sonatype.org
  /content/repositories/releases
^
  -DgroupId=lift.cookbook ^
  -DartifactId=chap01-mvn ^
  -Dversion=1.0
```

   After running the previous command, Maven will start to download all the required libraries to create the project.

2. Once the download is complete, Maven will ask you to confirm some information about the project. Confirm them by typing Y and pressing **return**.

3. Change the following tags in the `pom.xml` file:

   From:

   ```
   <scala.version>2.9.1</scala.version>
   ```

   To:

   ```
   <scala.version>2.10</scala.version>
   ```

   From:

   ```
   <artifactId>lift-mapper_2.9.1</artifactId>
   ```

   To:

   ```
   <artifactId>lift-mapper_2.10</artifactId>
   ```

   From:

   ```
   <artifactId>lift-jquery-module_2.9.1</artifactId>
   <version>2.5-2.0</version>
   ```

   To:

   ```
   <artifactId>lift-jquery-module_2.5_2.10</artifactId>
   <version>2.4</version>
   ```

   From:

   ```
   <groupId>org.scala-tools</groupId>
   <artifactId>maven-scala-plugin</artifactId>
   <version>2.15.2</version>
   ```

   To:

   ```
   <groupId>net.alchim31.maven</groupId>
   <artifactId>scala-maven-plugin</artifactId>
   <version>3.1.5</version>
   ```

   From:

   ```
   <groupId>org.mortbay.jetty</groupId>
   <artifactId>maven-jetty-plugin</artifactId>
   <version>6.1.26</version>
   ```

   To:

   ```
   <groupId>org.eclipse.jetty</groupId>
   <artifactId>jetty-maven-plugin</artifactId>
   ```

4. When you have finished editing the `pom.xml` file, open a cmd window, go to the folder containing the `pom.xml` file, and run the following command to update and compile the project:

   ```
   mvn compile
   ```

5. Once Maven finishes the compilation, you will be able to start the application by running the following command:

```
mvn jetty:run
```

6. Now that you have the application up and running, you can access `http://localhost:8080` in your favorite browser, and you should see a welcome page similar to the following:

How it works...

When you create a project using the Lift archetype, you get a fully working application containing everything you need to build your own application. This means that Maven will create an application with its default directory structure, a `pom.xml` file, with everything needed by the sample application. It will also include the jetty plugin that will allow us to run the application by running the `jetty:run` command.

The application created by Maven is a sample application that contains Blueprint CSS and a Mapper model. One more thing to notice is that this archetype also includes plugins for IntelliJ IDEA and Scala IDE.

See also

To learn more about Maven, please go to `http://maven.apache.org/`.

Defining a SiteMap

Lift offers several ways for programmers to define which pages their applications will have. SiteMap is one of these ways. Besides defining the pages of your application, you can also control the access of each URL. This means that you can, for example, control whether a URL will have access restrictions or not and even control the restriction level of any given URL.

What does this mean? This means that you can think of SiteMap as the defined structure of your application containing every URL that will be accessible and the policies that are applied for each one of them.

Another thing that SiteMap does is automatic mapping between URLs and XHTML templates.

In this recipe, we will see how to configure SiteMap for a simple application. For this, let's suppose we want to create an application to store and manage contacts.

We will need one URL for each of the following actions:

- List contacts
- Create contacts
- Edit contacts
- Delete contacts
- View contacts' details

Getting ready

Copy the contents of the `lift_blank` folder from the `scala_29` folder to a new directory called `contacts-app`.

How to do it...

Carry out the following steps:

1. Edit the `Boot.scala` file by adding a function, `LocParam`, just before the declaration of the `entries` value:

   ```
   val canManage_? = If(() => {
     true
   }, () => RedirectResponse("/"))
   ```

   This is to verify whether the user accessing the URL has management permission and is allowed to access it.

2. Then, add another `LocParam` to check whether the user has administrative privileges:

   ```
   val isAdmin_? = If(() => {
     false
   }, () => RedirectWithState("/contacts/list",
     MessageState("Authorized personnel only" ->
       NoticeType.Warning)))
   ```

3. After creating the functions, we'll define SiteMap by adding new menu items between the `Menu.i("Home")` / `"index"` and the `Menu(Loc("Static"`, ... entries.

Menu items that need to be added are as follows:

```
Menu.i("List Contacts") / "contacts" / "list",
Menu.i("Create") / "contacts" / "create" >> canManage_?,
Menu.i("Edit") / "contacts" / "edit" >> canManage_?,
Menu.i("Delete") / "contacts" / "delete" >> isAdmin_?,
Menu.i("View") / "contacts" / "view" >> canManage_?,
```

4. Create a folder called `contacts` inside the `webapp` folder.

5. Create five HTML files, one for each menu item defined in SiteMap:

   ❑ `list.html`

   ❑ `create.html`

   ❑ `edit.html`

   ❑ `delete.html`

   ❑ `view.html`

6. Then run the application and go to the URL `http://localhost:8080` in your browser. The following screen will be displayed:

How it works...

Lift will build the SiteMap object during the application boot process as a result of the invocation of the method, `LiftRules.setSiteMap`.

When a user tries to access, for example /`contacts/list`, Lift will use SiteMap to decide whether the resource is defined or not by matching the URL against the link list defined by the menu entries in SiteMap. Since we've defined it, Lift will serve the page to the user. However, if the user tries to access /`contacts/lists`, the match will fail and Lift will return a 404 error.

We still need to understand what the `LocParam` functions are that were mentioned in steps 1 and 2. `LocParam` is something that modifies how Lift handles the given entry of SiteMap. In our case, it is a function that redirects the user to a different URL if the condition being tested fails. So, if someone tries to access `/contacts/create`, Lift will execute the `canManage_?` function after matching the URL. If the function returns `true`, Lift will serve the page to the user; otherwise, it will redirect the user to `/`. The same logic applies to the view and edit URLs.

The same logic applies to the delete link; the only difference being the fact that the `isAdmin_?` function not only redirects the user to `/`, but also passes a message that will be displayed in the page. This happens because we've used `If LocParam` that takes two arguments. The first is a test function. If it returns `true`, the page can be accessed; and if the return value is `false`, the result of evaluating the second parameter, `FailMsg`, will be sent to the browser.

There's more...

The `entries` variable is a list of menu items that will be processed when the application is started by Jetty.

Each menu item has a structure as shown in the following image.

- ▶ Unique identifier
- ▶ Link object
- ▶ Text
- ▶ Parameters

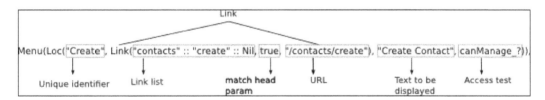

The unique identifier is used by Lift to keep a track of all the menu entries in SiteMap.

The Link contains the list that will be used to match the requested URL to check if it is defined or not.

The `match head` parameter, which is a Boolean value, defines whether Lift will match the exact URL or everything beginning with the given path. Notice that if you pass `true`, Lift will serve URLs containing `/contacts/create` or `/contacts/create/*`, where `*` is any HTML file existing inside `webapps/contacts/create`. If no such folder exists, Lift will return a 404 error. If you pass `false`, Lift will only serve `/contacts/create` and will return the 404 error for any other URL containing `/contacts/create`.

The URL that will be used to create the link on the page will be the value rendered in the `href` attribute of the anchor tag, `<a href={url}>...</a>`.

`text` is the text that will be shown when the link is displayed.

The parameters are functions, `LocParam`, that you want to execute when rendering the link or accessing the page.

Lift comes with several types of the `LocParam` functions, such as `MenuCssClass` to add a CSS class to the Menu and `Title` to define the title of the page.

See also

To learn more about SiteMap, Menu, and the `LocParam` functions, please go to `https://www.assembla.com/wiki/show/liftweb/SiteMap`.

Logging using logback

Logback is a log engine that is intended to be a better version of the popular log4j. You might want to check the project website to understand the reasons you should consider Logback over log4j. But, you might ask why we need a log engine at all?

Logging is a useful tool that allows us to track what happens with the applications we build that are running on environments which we, as developers, cannot easily debug. That's why it is important that the tools we use to build applications support logging in an easy way. Lift does support logging in an easy and flexible manner. So, let us see how to log and what happens with our application.

Downloading the example code

You can download the example code files for all Packt books you have purchased from your account at `http://www.packtpub.com`. If you purchased this book elsewhere, you can visit `http://www.packtpub.com/support` and register to have the files e-mailed directly to you.

Getting ready

We will use the code from the last section to re-use the SiteMap we have defined.

How to do it...

Don't worry if you don't fully understand the following code. We will get back to it later in the book.

1. Create a new Scala class called `ListUser` inside the snippet package with the following code:

```scala
class ListUser extends Logger {
  def log(text: String) {
    text match {
      case str if str.length == 0 =>
        error("user with no name")
      case str if str == "Forbidden" =>
        warn("this user shouldn't have access")
      case str =>
        debug("User name: " + str)
    }
  }
  def list = {
    val users = List("John", "Sarah", "Peter", "Sam", "",
      "Forbidden")
    info("listing users")
    "li .name *" #> users.map {
      user => {
        log(user)
        Text(user)
      }
    }
  }
}
```

2. Add the following HTML snippet in `/webapp/contacts/list.html`:

```html
<ul data-lift="ListUser.list">
  <li class="name"><!-- user names will be in here --></li>
</ul>
```

3. Change the `code.snippet` logger in `src/main/resources/logback.xml` to debug the level as follows:

```xml
<logger name="code.snippet" level="debug" />
```

4. Start the application and go to `http://localhost:8080/contacts/list` in your browser.

In your browser, you will see, a page similar to the one shown in the following screenshot:

In the SBT console, you will see a log similar to the following screenshot:

```
> 11:58:31.880 [qtp1551646784-554  /contacts/list] INFO  code.snippet.ListUser - listing users
11:58:31.971 [qtp1551646784-554 - /contacts/list] DEBUG code.snippet.ListUser - User name: John
11:58:31.971 [qtp1551646784-554 - /contacts/list] DEBUG code.snippet.ListUser - User name: Sarah
11:58:31.971 [qtp1551646784-554 - /contacts/list] DEBUG code.snippet.ListUser - User name: Peter
11:58:31.971 [qtp1551646784-554 - /contacts/list] DEBUG code.snippet.ListUser - User name: Sam
11:58:31.972 [qtp1551646784-554 - /contacts/list] ERROR code.snippet.ListUser - user with no name
11:58:31.972 [qtp1551646784-554 - /contacts/list] WARN  code.snippet.ListUser - this user should haven't access
```

How it works...

We configured the log in the `logback.xml` file. You might notice that there was an appender already configured. Appenders are the components that actually do the task of writing log events. There are several types of appenders and one of them is the **ConsoleAppender** that just prints the log entries in the standard output—the console in this case.

The class `ListUser` is a Lift snippet that traverses the list of strings defined by variable users. For each string, it does two things:

 ▸ Invokes the `log` method

 ▸ Adds the string inside the `li` tag

Then it returns the modified HTML to be rendered in the browser.

The `log` method will create a log entry with different log levels depending on the string's content, by invoking the method from the `Logger` trait which includes `info`, `debug`, `error`, `warning`, and so on.

The `Logger` trait's methods are accessible from the snippet because we mixed them in our snippet by extending them using `extends Logger`. Then the snippet is invoked by the instruction `ListUser.list` that we added in the `data-lift` attribute in the HTML file.

There's more...

When you use the `Logger` trait, Lift will create one logger per class or object. That is why we can see the object or class where the log entry was created. You can see in our example that the log was created by the ListUser snippet by extending the trait.

This is a nice feature since we can have more control of how our application creates the log entries. We can, for example, set packages with different log levels. As you can see in the `logback.xml` file, the `code.snippet` has the debug level while `net.liftweb` has the warn level and `bootstrap.liftweb` has the info level.

Logback is not the only log engine available. If you want to use log4j, you will need to change the dependency in the `build.sbt` file from:

```
"ch.qos.logback"    % "logback-classic"    % "1.0.6",
```

To:

```
"org.slf4j" % "slf4j-log4j12" % "1.6.1",
```

Also, you will need to create `src/main/resources/log4j.xml`, which is log4j's configuration file.

See also

▶ You can find more about log4j at the following URL:

```
http://logging.apache.org/log4j/1.2/
```

▶ Check this URL if you want to learn more about Logback:

```
http://logback.qos.ch/
```

▶ At last, you can find more information about other ways to use Lift's log engine, such as how to create a singleton logger object for the entire application, as shown here:

```
https://www.assembla.com/spaces/liftweb/wiki/Logging
```

Sending e-mails using Gmail's SMTP server

It does not matter if you are building your company website, an application that will be used only inside the company you work at, or an e-commerce solution. Eventually, you will need to send e-mails. It is fair to say that every web application has the need, at some point, to send e-mails.

In this recipe, we will learn how to send plain text e-mails using Gmail's SMTP server.

Getting ready

You can use the code of the examples we have used in the previous recipe, or you can start a new project.

How to do it...

Carry out the following steps:

1. You will need to add the following properties into `src/main/resources/default.props`:

    ```
    mail.user=your_email@gmail.com
    mail.password=your_password
    ```

2. Change the `mail.user` and `mail.password` properties to match your Gmail account.

3. Then create a method in the `Boot` class to configure the `Mailer` object as follows:

    ```
    def configureMailer() {
      import javax.mail{PasswordAuthentication, Authenticator}

      System.setProperty("mail.smtp.starttls.enable", "true")
      System.setProperty("mail.smtp.ssl.enable", "true")
      System.setProperty("mail.smtp.host", "smtp.gmail.com")
      System.setProperty("mail.smtp.auth", "true")

      Mailer.authenticator = for {
        user <- Props.get("mail.user")
        pass <- Props.get("mail.password")
      } yield new Authenticator {
        override def getPasswordAuthentication =
        new PasswordAuthentication(user, pass)
      }
    }
    ```

4. Then, you need to call the `configureMailer` method from within the `boot` method:

    ```
    def boot {
      // where to search snippet
      LiftRules.addToPackages("code")

      configureMailer()
      ….
    }
    ```

    Now, we have the `Mailer` object configured, and we are ready to send e-mails.

5. Inside the lib package `src/main/scala/code/`, create an object called `SendEmail` that will be responsible for sending e-mails:

```scala
import net.liftweb.util.Mailer
import net.liftweb.util.Mailer._

object SendEmail {
  def send_!(from: String,
    recipient: String,
    subject: String,
  body: String) {
    val mailTypes = List(PlainMailBodyType(body),
      To(recipient))

    Mailer.msgSendImpl (
      From(from),
      Subject(subject),
    mailTypes)
  }
}
```

6. At last, we will create a snippet to render a link to send e-mails when clicked. For this, you will need to create a class called `EmailSnippet` inside the snippet package, `src/main/scala/code/`:

```scala
import net.liftweb.http.SHtml
import net.liftweb.util. Helpers._
import code.lib.SendEmail
import xml.Text
import net.liftweb.util.Props

class SEmail {
  def sendNow() = {
    SendEmail.send_!(
      Props.get("mail.user").get,
      "to_email@example.com",
      "Sending e-mail using GMail",
      "Here is the body content."
    )
  }

  def sendEmail = {
    "*" #> SHtml.link("#", () => sendNow(), Text("Send
      e-mail"))
  }
}
```

7. Change `to_email@example.com` to match your Gmail account.

8. You will also need to create the following menu item in the entries list, just after the index entry:

```
Menu.i("Send Email") / "send"
```

9. Create a file called `send.html` inside `src/main/webapp` as follows:

```
<!DOCTYPE html PUBLIC "-//W3C//DTD XHTML 1.0
  Transitional//EN"
    "http://www.w3.org/TR/xhtml1/DTD/
      xhtml1-transitional.dtd">
<html xmlns="http://www.w3.org/1999/xhtml">
  <head>
    <meta content="text/html; charset=UTF-8"
      http-equiv="content-type"/>
    <title>Home</title>
  </head>
  <body class="lift:content_id=main">
    <div id="main"
      class="lift:surround?with=default;at=content">
    <h2>Sending e-mail using GMail's SMTP server.</h2>

    <p>
      <span data-lift="EmailSnippet.sendEmail"><!-- there
        will be a button here --></span>
    </p>
    </div>
  </body>
</html>
```

10. Start the application and go to `http://localhost:8080/send`.

    You should see a page containing a link called **Send e-mail**, similar to the following screenshot:

11. Click on the link to send the email, and you will receive an email in your Gmail inbox.

How it works...

First of all, we have set a few mail properties that will be used by the Java Mail API, such as `mail.smtp.ssl.enable` and `mail.smtp.starttls.enable`. These properties will enable SSL and TLS, meaning that we will use a secure channel to send the e-mail, and `mail.smtp.host` to set the SMTP server address. Then, we set `mail.smtp.auth` to `true` to use the SMTP authentication.

The next thing we did was to create an authenticator to use the `Mailer` object.

 `Mailer` is a built-in Lift object that contains utilities to send e-mails.

When creating the authenticator, we used the `Props` object to get the user and password values from the `default.props` file.

 Props is a Lift helper object that can be used to get values from properties files.

Then, we created the `EmailSnippet` class that creates a link which when clicked, invokes the `sendNow()` method. This method has no parameters and calls the SendEmail's `send_!` method, passing information such as `from`, `to`, `subject`, and `body` that will be used to send the e-mail. We had to wrap the call to `send_!` to keep the code easy to read. Then SendEmail's `send_!` invokes `Mailer` object's `sendMail` method, which is the method that will send the e-mail.

There's more...

Why did we do all of this in the `Boot` class? Well, we just needed to configure the `Mailer` object once. This is because it's a singleton, which means that only one instance of the object will be created, and we can use it throughout the application once it is configured. So, `Boot` is the perfect place to do this, since it is called only once when the server, in our case Jetty, is starting the application.

Note that we configured the `Mailer` object in a programmatic way. However, if you want to use **The Java Naming and Directory Interface** (**JNDI**) to configure the `Mailer` object, you will need to do two things.

By using JNDI to configure the `Mailer` object, you can rely on the fact that the configurations will be set on the server; your application only needs to know the JNDI name to be able to use a given resource. This means that if you need to change the application server where your application will run, you won't have problems with different settings causing your application to break.

1. First you need to call the following code instead of using the `configureMailer()` method:

```
Mailer.jndiName = Full("mail/Session")
```

2. Second, you need to configure the server to provide a mail session via JNDI. You do this by creating a file called `jetty-env.xml` inside the `WEB-INF` folder:

```
<!DOCTYPE Configure PUBLIC "-//Jetty//Configure//EN"
  "http://www.eclipse.org/jetty/configure.dtd">
<Configure class="org.eclipse.jetty.webapp.WebAppContext">
  <New id="mail"
    class="org.eclipse.jetty.plus.jndi.Resource">
    <Arg>mail/Session</Arg>
    <Arg>
      <New
        class="org.eclipse.jetty.jndi.factories.
          MailSessionReference">
        <Set name="user">your_email@gmail.com</Set>
        <Set name="password">your_password</Set>
        <Set name="properties">
          <New class="java.util.Properties">
            <Put name="mail.transport.protocol">smtp</Put>
            <Put name="mail.smtp.host">smtp.gmail.com</Put>
            <Put name="mail.smtp.auth">true</Put>
            <Put
               name="mail.smtp.starttls.enable">true</Put>
            <Put name="mail.smtp.ssl.enable">true</Put>
            <Put name="mail.debug">true</Put>
          </New>
        </Set>
      </New>
    </Arg>
  </New>
</Configure>
```

See also

You can get more information about the Mailer objects at the following addresses:

▶ `https://www.assembla.com/spaces/liftweb/wiki/Mailer`
▶ `http://exploring.liftweb.net/master/index-F.html`

2
Working with HTML

In this chapter, we will cover the following topics:

- ▶ Transforming HTML elements using their IDs
- ▶ Creating an HTML list using CSS selectors
- ▶ Creating an HTML table with dynamically defined columns
- ▶ Nesting snippets
- ▶ Dynamic menu rendering
- ▶ Localizing templates
- ▶ Testing snippets using Specs2
- ▶ Creating custom error pages
- ▶ Sending JavaScript commands from the server
- ▶ Invoking server-side functions from the client

Introduction

In the previous chapter, we learned how to create a Lift project using both SBT and Maven. We also learned how to do basic things such as sending e-mails and configuring the SiteMap.

We also created few pages and examples to demonstrate some of the features of this amazing framework called Lift.

As, Lift is a framework used to build websites and applications using Scala, we need to learn how to create pages, how to manipulate HTML to create dynamic pages, how to localize our website, and a lot of other useful things that are necessary while building a website.

Another neat feature that you will see in the following recipes, is that Lift templates are designer friendly. That is because bindings between HTML and Lift snippets are made by adding markups inside the data-lift attribute of HTML tags. Since this is all you need to create the binding, your HTML file will be valid and designers working on the same project won't have a hard time editing them.

These are the topics that we will learn in this chapter.

Transforming HTML elements using their IDs

Suppose you are building a page and you want to show some unique information, such as the user name and the total amount of a shopping cart; what would you do?

You will probably need to add the information that you want to show into some tags with a unique identifier.

This is exactly what we will learn to do in this recipe.

Getting ready

You can use the code from the examples we used in the recipes of the previous chapter or you can start a new project.

How to do it...

An HTML element can be transformed by using the following steps:

1. Add the following code into the index.html file:

```
<div data-lift="Calculator.plus">
   2 + 2 = <span id="result">some number</span>
</div>
```

2. Create a Calculator object inside the snippet folder with the following code:

```
import net.liftweb.util.BindHelpers._
object Calculator {
   def plus = "#result *" #> (2 + 2)
}
```

3. Start the application and access `http://localhost:8080`. You should see a page similar to the following screenshot:

How it works...

When working on a Lift application, the `data-lift` attribute in an HTML tag will search for a snippet to do the job.

> If Lift does not find a `snippet` object or if the `snippet` object doesn't have the invoked method, Lift will show an error message when you try to access the page.

The text before the dot, `Calculator`, is the name of the snippet class or object and the text after the dot, `plus`, is the method that will be invoked.

In this example, we are telling Lift to invoke the `Calculator` object's `plus` method. Let's take a look at the `plus` method to see what it does.

The `plus` method has no parameters and its return type is `CssSel`.

The `CssSel` trait performs HTML transformations using CSS selectors. Its job is to get some HTML (`scala.xml.NodeSeq`), transform it, and then return the transformed HTML (a new `NodeSeq`).

Therefore, what is really happening here is that the `plus` method gets the content of the `div` tag and changes it.

When the `plus` method is invoked, it will search for the HTML tag that has `id` equal to `"result"`, and change it by replacing the tag with `result` as the value of `id`, with the result of the evaluation of the expression $2 + 2$.

You can see this by looking at the resulting HTML in your browser. The original snippet was:

```
<div data-lift="Calculator.plus">
  2 + 2 = <span id="result">some number</span>
</div>
```

It was then changed to:

```
<div>
  2 + 2 = <span id="result">4</span>
</div>
```

Another thing you'll notice, is that there is no mention of the snippet in the resulting HTML.

See also

▸   To learn more about CSS selectors, please visit the following URL: `http://simply.liftweb.net/index-7.10.html`

Creating an HTML list using CSS selectors

In the previous recipe, we learned how to show data that should be unique using a CSS selector and the `id` attribute of HTML tags. However, there are a lot of times when we need to show collections of data, such as the names of students in a given classroom, the list of items in a shopping cart, or a list of whatever else you can think of.

This is exactly what we will learn how to do in this recipe.

Getting ready

You can use the code from the examples we used in the previous recipe or you can start a new project.

How to do it...

A HTML list can be created by following these steps:

1. Add the following section in the `index.html` file:

    ```
    <div data-lift="Animals.list">
      <ul>
        <li><span class="name"></span> - <span
          class="sname"></span></li>
      </ul>
    </div>
    ```

2. Create a file called `Animals.scala` in the `snippets` folder with the following code:

    ```
    import net.liftweb.util.BindHelpers._
    import xml.Text
    ```

```
object Animals {
  def list = {
    val animals = List(
      ("Dog", "(Canis lupus familiaris)"),
      ("Cat", "(Felis catus)"),
      ("Giraffe", "(Giraffa camelopardalis)"),
      ("Lion", "(Panthera leo)"),
      ("Horse", "(Equus ferus caballus)")
    )

    "li *" #> animals.map {
      a =>
        ".name *" #> Text(a._1) &
        ".sname *" #> Text(a._2)


    }
  }
}
```

3. Start the application and access `http://localhost:8080`. You'll see a page with a list of common names and scientific names of five animals, as shown in the following screenshot:

How it works...

There are no secrets in HTML. We added the markup to invoke the snippet that will render the HTML file. We did this by adding `l:Animals.list` in the `div` tag.

We also added two `span` tags, one with class `name` and the other with class `sname` to mark where we want the content to be added when Lift transforms the HTML.

But, how did Lift change the original HTML file into a list of animal names?

As I said before, we tell Lift to invoke a method in a snippet when we add `l:.....` inside the class attribute of a given HTML tag. In this case, we invoked the method `list` of the snippet `Animals`.

This method receives a `NodeSeq` object, creates a list of tuples, and then changes the content of the `<li>` tag for each element in the animal list by changing the content of any tag with the `name` or `sname` classes. What we are saying to Lift is that, for each element in my list, create an `<li>` tag and put the first element of the tuple into a tag containing the `name` class and the tuple's second element into a tag containing the `sname` class.

You can see that the `span` tags are in the final HTML rendered by Lift. Why didn't Lift remove the `span` tags as it did in the previous recipe?

As it happens, we used `#result` as the CSS selector in the first example and `li *`, `.name *`, and `.sname *` in this one. The difference is just that of one character; that is, `*`.

The difference between using the character `*` and not using it is that when you use it, you tell Lift to change the *content of the tag* that matches with the CSS selector, and when you don't use it, you tell Lift to replace the tag itself. While `".name *"` `#> Text(...)` replaces the content of a tag containing the class `name` with `some text`, `".name"` `#> Text(...)` replaces *the tag* containing the class `name` with `some text`. So, the HTML for the first case will be `<span class="name">some text</name>`, while for the second, it will be just `some text`.

There's more...

You should note that, in the first recipe, we passed an integer as an argument for the `#>` method, while in this recipe's example, we've passed a list of `CssSel`. You might wonder how this is possible.

As it turns out, Lift comes with several transformation rules that are each passed as an implicit parameter to the `#>` method. These transformation rules "know" how to convert the parameter passed to the `#>` method to the correct type.

For example, if you pass an integer, the `intTransform` method will be used, and if you pass a list of strings, the `iterableStringTransform` method will be used.

Another neat and useful tool to try out while developing a Lift application is the CSS selector in the Scala REPL. You can open the Scala REPL by entering the `console` command in the SBT session.

Once you get the Scala REPL, import the content of Lift's `Helper` object, `net.liftweb.util.Helper`, and you are ready to start experimenting.

As a quick example, type the following code in the Scala REPL:

```scala
scala> val transformSpanContent = "span *" #> "Some Text"
scala> transformSpanContent(<span>this text will be replaced</span>)
```

You'll get this result:

```scala
res0: scala.xml.NodeSeq = NodeSeq(<span>Some text</span>)
```

As you can see, we did a quick experiment to check what happens with a `scala.xml.NodeSeq` object after being transformed by the CssSel we've defined.

See also

Visit `http://simply.liftweb.net/index-7.10.html` to learn more about CSS selectors.

Creating an HTML table with dynamically defined columns

We often need to display tabular data while building websites. Sometimes we know beforehand all of the columns we will need to display, but sometimes we don't.

Handling tabular data with dynamically defined columns is a bit harder than handling data with a fixed number of columns because you will need to dynamically render the columns and the rows. On the other hand, when dealing with a fixed number of columns, you need to render just the rows.

I chose to work with dynamically defined columns for two reasons. First, it is more complex, and secondly, once you learn how to deal with dynamically defined columns, you will be able to work on the simpler case; that is, fixed columns.

Getting ready

First, we are going to create the HTML table. It's regular HTML—meaning that it has no special tags or any markup that is not HTML markup—with a `thead` section to hold the column headers and a `tbody` section to hold the data, and of course, it will invoke a `Lift` snippet.

1. Create a new project.
2. Create a table as follows:

```
<table data-lift="Table.dynamic">
  <thead>
    <tr>
      <th></th>
    </tr>
  </thead>
  <tbody>
    <tr>
      <td></td>
    </tr>
  </tbody>
</table>
```

How to do it...

The snippet structure should look familiar to you at this point, but there are a couple of things to learn. Let's check what the code looks like and then we'll see how it does its magic.

1. Create a snippet with the following code:

```
import net.liftweb.util.Helpers._
object Table {
  def dynamic = {
    val headers = (1 to 10)
    // creates a 10 x 10 matrix
    val table = headers.map(n => (1 to 10).map(in => n *
      in))

    "th *" #> headers
    &
    "tbody tr *"*" #> table.map {
      r => {
        "td *" #> r
      }
    }
  }
}
```

2. Start the app and access `http://localhost:8080`. You should see a screen similar to the one in the following screenshot:

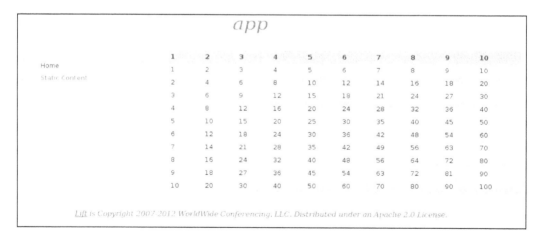

	1	2	3	4	5	6	7	8	9	10
Home	1	2	3	4	5	6	7	8	9	10
Static Content	2	4	6	8	10	12	14	16	18	20
	3	6	9	12	15	18	21	24	27	30
	4	8	12	16	20	24	28	32	36	40
	5	10	15	20	25	30	35	40	45	50
	6	12	18	24	30	36	42	48	54	60
	7	14	21	28	35	42	49	56	63	70
	8	16	24	32	40	48	56	64	72	80
	9	18	27	36	45	54	63	72	81	90
	10	20	30	40	50	60	70	80	90	100

How it works...

There is nothing new in the HTML, just the call to the snippet using the `data-lift` notation, and we were still able to create a table with a dynamic number of columns and rows. This is amazing and shows how powerful CSS selectors are.

All the magic happens in the snippet, so let's take a look at it. As far as one can tell, it's a regular snippet with no super powers, and this is the case indeed.

There are two things that made this task feasible. The first one is the `&` operator which lets us perform chain binding operations. In this case, we chained together the `th` and `tbody` bindings. The second is the nesting of bindings. If you take a closer look at the `tbody` binding, you'll see that we first bound the `tr` tags and in this binding we created another one for the `td` tags.

So, what we are doing here is telling Lift to create a table's header columns with the `th` binding, just as we did for the list in the previous recipe; each element of the collection headers will generate a `th` tag. Then, using the same technique, we told Lift to create a row for each element of the table collection. But, each element of the table collection is another collection. Look at the following figure, and you will see why we nest another bind inside the `tr` binding. The nested binding uses the same technique as the previous binds, `th` and `tr`. So, it will create a list of `td` elements.

This is how we were able to create a table with both columns and rows dynamically defined.

See also

- The *Transforming HTML elements using their IDs* recipe
- The *Creating an HTML list using CSS selectors* recipe
- The Simply Lift website: `http://simply.liftweb.net/index-7.10.html`
- The Exploring Lift website: `http://exploring.liftweb.net/master/index-5.html#toc-Subsection-5.3.2`
- The Assembla webpage for Binding via CSS Selectors: `https://www.assembla.com/spaces/liftweb/wiki/Binding_via_CSS_Selectors`

Nesting snippets

Snippets are lazily evaluated, which means that the `Inner` snippet will not be invoked until the `Outer` snippet is evaluated. By using this neat feature, we can nest snippet invocations in our HTML templates, and thus gain a powerful tool to dynamically generate HTML with a fine-grained control. For example, you can use this feature to show different things to your users depending on whether they are logged in or not and on their authorization level. We'll learn how to do this in this recipe.

Getting ready

Create a new project and add the following designer-friendly HTML code into the `index.html` file to invoke the snippet and trigger all of the mechanisms to render snippets recursively:

```
<div data-lift="Outer.choose">
  <div class="inner-div"></div>
</div>
```

How to do it...

Nesting snippets can be done by following these steps:

1. Create a file called `Outer.scala` in the `snippet` package with the following content:

```
import net.liftweb.util.Helpers._
import net.liftweb.http.S
import net.liftweb.util.BasicTypesHelpers._
import net.liftweb.common.Full

object Outer {
  def choose = {
    val loggedIn = S.param("loggedin").flatMap(asBoolean)
```

```
        loggedIn match {
          case Full(b) if b => ".inner-div [class+]" #>
            "lift:Inner.logged"
          case _ => ".inner-div [class+]" #>
            "lift:Inner.nonlogged"
        }
      }
    }
```

After building the `Outer` snippet, we'll build the `Inner` one.

2. Create a file called `Inner.scala` in the `snippet` package with the following content:

```
import net.liftweb.util.Helpers._

object Inner {
  def logged = {
    "div *" #> "Should only be visible when user is
      logged in"
  }

  def nonlogged = {
    "div *" #> "Should only be visible when user is not
      logged in"
  }
}
```

3. Access the following URLs to test this example:

   ❏ `http://localhost:8080?loggedin=true`

   ❏ `http://localhost:8080?loggedin=false`

   ❏ `http://localhost:8080`

You will see the following output, as shown in the following screenshot:

How it works...

As you can see, the only snippet invocation in the HTML file is the invocation of the `Outer` snippet; the rest of the HTML is just plain HTML markup—nothing special or new. But we have two snippets and only one invocation in the HTML file. As it turns out, when Lift starts to process HTML, it will find the snippet invocation and will pass the HTML code to it.

The `Outer` snippet will check for the presence of the `loggedin` parameter. It does this by using the `param` method of the `S` object; it then uses this parameter to choose which snippet will be rendered next.

S is an object that holds the HTTP requests/responses and HTTP session state.

When we invoke the `S` object's `param` method, it will try to get a query string—having the key passed as parameter to the `param` method—from the URL.

The `S.param` method returns `Box[String]`; it will return `Full[String]` if it successfully gets the query string, or `Empty` if the key doesn't exist.

`Box` is a container class that can be empty or full. If `Box` contains a value different from `null`, the box's value is `Full(value)`; otherwise, the value of `Box` will be `Empty`. Other possible values for an empty box are `Failure` and `ParamFailure`, which can include the reason why the box is empty.

If the parameter is true, it will append `lift:Inner.logged` to the `class` attribute of the `div` tag with `inner-div` as value of the `class` attribute; if the parameter is false or non-existent, it will append `lift:Inner.nonlogged` to the `class` attribute.

How does Lift know that we want to append something to the `class` attribute of a tag? By using the `[attr+]` selector, we tell Lift to append the result of the right-hand side of the `#>` operator to the `tag` attribute. Since we used `[class+]`, we told Lift to append `lift:...` to the `class` attribute.

You can read more about CSS Selector Transforms at `http://simply.liftweb.net/index-7.10.html`.

Once the `Outer` snippet finishes its job, the transformed HTML—if the value of the `loggedin` parameter is `true`—will look like the following code:

```
<div>
  <div class="inner l:Inner.logged"></div>
</div>
```

We no longer have the invocation of the `Outer` snippet. The HTML will now invoke the `Inner` snippet, which is a snippet that will render some text inside the `div` tag. The final HTML will look the following code:

```
<div>
  <div class="inner">
    Should only be visible when user is logged in
  </div>
</div>
```

What we did is:

1. Invoke the `Outer` snippet.

2. Choose which snippet should be called, based on some condition.

3. Return HTML that contains in itself an invocation to another snippet—the `Inner` snippet.

4. Process the HTML in the `Inner` snippet.

5. Return the transformed HTML.

That's all you need to create nested calls to snippets in Lift.

See also

You can read more about snippets at:

- ▶ http://simply.liftweb.net/index-3.4.html
- ▶ http://simply.liftweb.net/index-7.1.html#sec:snippets

Dynamic menu rendering

Menus are an important part of an application. They show a hierarchical structure and how the application is organized. Users will use them to navigate through the application.

Lift does offer a good built-in snippet for creating menus, as I briefly said before. In this recipe, I'll show you how to use this snippet to create complex menu structures, and how to render them with fine-grained control.

Getting ready

Create a new project and add the following code in the `Boot` class to create the SiteMap:

```
Val isAdmin_? = If(() => {
  S.param("admin").flatMap(asBoolean).openOr(false)
  }, () => RedirectWithState("/", MessageState(
  "Authorized personnel only" -> NoticeType.Warning))
)
val entries = List(
  Menu.i("Home") / "index" >> LocGroup("content"), // the
    simple way to declare a menu

  Menu("Admin") / "admin" >> Hidden
  submenus(
    Menu(Loc("List", List("list"), "List Contacts",
      isAdmin_?, LocGroup("admin"))),
    Menu(Loc("Create", List("create"), "Create Contact",
      isAdmin_?, LocGroup("admin"))),
    Menu(Loc("Edit", List("edit"), "Edit Contact",
      isAdmin_?, LocGroup("admin"))),
    Menu(Loc("Delete", List("delete"), "Delete Contact",
      isAdmin_?, LocGroup("admin"))),
    Menu(Loc("View", List("view"), "View Contact",
      isAdmin_?, LocGroup("admin")))
  ),
  Menu("Search") / "search" >> LocGroup("content"),
  Menu("Contact Us") / "contact" >> LocGroup("footer"),
  Menu("About Us") / "about" >> LocGroup("footer"),

  // more complex because this menu allows anything in the
  // /static path to be visible
  Menu(Loc("Static", Link(List("static"), true,
    "/static/index"),
"Static Content", LocGroup("content"))))
```

How to do it...

Rendering a menu dynamically can be done by following these steps:

1. In the `default.html` file, change the invocation to the `MenuBuilder` snippet from `<span class="lift:Menu.builder"></span>` to `<span class="lift:Menu.builder?group=content"></span>`.

2. Add the following code snippet after the `div` tag with `content` as the value of the `id` field:

```
<div>
  <span class="lift:Menu.builder?group=admin"></span>
</div>
```

3. Then remove the `h4` tag and the tag within the `div` tag and containing the class `last`, and add the following code:

```
<span class="lift:Menu.builder?group=footer"></span>
```

4. Start the application and access `http://localhost:8080` and `http://localhost:8080?admin=true`. You should see a page similar to the one shown in the following screenshot:

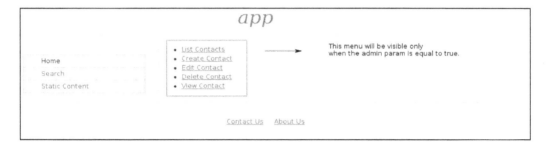

How it works...

I'll start with the Scala code because it will be easier to first understand what this code does before trying to understand the HTML code. In fact, once you grasp how the SiteMap was built and how it works, the HTML code becomes pretty simple.

If you pay attention to the code, you'll see that we are creating a list of menu items, just like we discussed earlier, but this code is different from the previous one as it uses `LocGroup` and `hidden`, and has a submenu. The former can be used to place together menu items in logical groups, while the latter creates hierarchical menu structures, like the one appearing in the following screenshot:

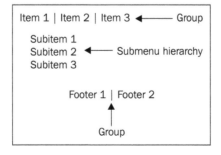

We used the `hidden` property to prevent the menu from being shown on the page when the `MenuBuilder` snippet gets invoked. The submenu is shown only for users who are administrators. We did this by invoking the `isAdmin_?` function. This function evaluates the `admin` parameter and returns `true` or `false` depending upon the value of the parameter which could either be `true` or `false`. If the function returns `true`, the menu item will be both visible and accessible. However, it will not be visible if the function returns `false`, and if you try to access the URL directly, Lift will call the `isAdmin_?` function, which will redirect the user to / if the function returns `false`.

We also used `LocGroup` to divide the SiteMap into three logical groups: `content`, `footer`, and `admin`. So, the SiteMap has three groups, and one of them is hidden and has a submenu that is only visible to users with the right credentials. We now need to understand how this structure is transformed into HTML by Lift.

Looking closely at the HTML snippet, you'll find invocations to the `MenuBuilder` snippet. But, we are not just invoking snippets here. We are invoking and passing parameters to them.

 You can pass parameters to snippets like you would with URL parameters—a question mark and a bunch of key-value pairs. For example, `?key1=value1&key2=value2....`

Lift uses these parameters as filters and will render only the items that have `LocGroup` specified by the parameter. When we say `?group=content`, we are telling Lift to render only the items with `LocGroup("content")`.

The final point to cover is the menu with `LocGroup("admin")` which we defined as `hidden`; a menu item defined as `hidden` is not rendered by Lift when the `MenuBuilder` snippet is invoked. If the menu item is not rendered, how will we access the items in the `admin` menu? As it turns out, the only item that is hidden is the one defined as `hidden`. Submenus are not affected. But we still want to let only users with the right credentials access the `admin` menu. To accomplish this, I created a function to tell Lift whether or not it should render the `admin` submenu items. Lift will only show it if we pass the `admin` parameter in the URL as `true`.

The `isAdmin_?` function is executed on every request and will be evaluated as `true` if you pass the `admin` parameter, and then Lift will render the menu. In this case, I used `LocGroup("admin")` to group all items together, so I can render them in a different area of the page.

 If you call `Menu.builder` with no parameter, Lift will render a complete SiteMap hierarchically. However, there is one catch—it will not render submenus hierarchically when `LocGroup` classes are used.

> ▸ The *Defining a SiteMap* recipe in *Chapter 1, Getting Started with Lift Basics*

Localizing templates

Sometimes, applications or websites we build need to support multiple languages. Lift supports this requirement by allowing us to localize templates, and offers a powerful yet simple way to choose which template to use when rendering the page.

In this recipe, we'll learn how to localize templates and texts that will be loaded dynamically for our applications or websites.

Getting ready

1. Create a new project and the following three bundle files in the `src/main/resources/i18n` folder:

   - The `resources.properties` file
   - The `resources_de.properties` file
   - The `resources_fr_FR.properties` file

2. The `resources.properties` file will have the following content:

   ```
   menu.home=Home
   menu.static=Static
   dynamic.text=Some dynamic text
   welcome.text= Welcome to your project!
   ```

3. While the file `resources_de.properties` will have the content shown in the following code:

   ```
   menu.home=Zuhause
   menu.static=Statisch
   dynamic.text=einige dynamischen Text
   welcome.text= Willkommen in Ihrem Projekt!
   ```

4. And the file `resources_fr_FR.properties` will have the content shown in the following code:

   ```
   menu.home=Page d'accueil
   menu.static=Statique
   dynamic.text=Un texte dynamique
   welcome.text= Bienvenue à votre projet!
   ```

How to do it...

1. We first need to tell Lift where it can find the files with the texts in different languages, also known as bundle files. You can do this by adding the following code in the `Boot` class:

```
LiftRules.resourceNames = "i18n/resources" ::
  LiftRules.resourceNames
```

2. Consider the following menu in the `Boot.scala` file:

```
Menu.i("Home") ….
…. "Static Content")))
```

You will need to change it to:

```
Menu("menu.home") ….
…. S ? "menu.static")))
```

We are also going to change the `index.html` file so that Lift can localize the static text.

3. Replace the content of the `div` tag with `main` as the value of the `id` field in the `index.html` file to:

```
<h2 data-lift="Loc.i">welcome.text</h2>

<p><span class="lift:Localization.dynamic"></span></p>
```

4. At last, we will need to create a file called `Localization.scala` in the snippet package to dynamically load localized text, as shown in the following code:

```
import net.liftweb.util.BindHelpers._
import net.liftweb.http.S

class Localization {
  def dynamic = {
    "*" #> S.?("dynamic.texttext")
  }
}
```

5. Start the application and access `http://localhost:8080`. You should see the page loaded in English, assuming English is the default language set in your browser, as shown in the following screenshot:

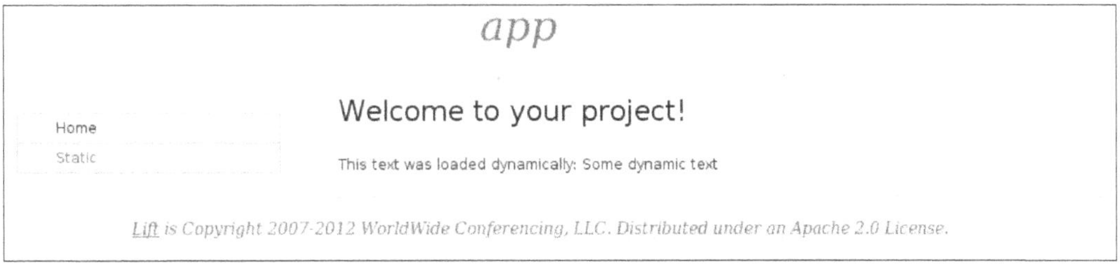

6. If you change your browser's language to German, you should see the page loaded in German, as shown in the following screenshot:

7. Finally, if you change your browser's language to French, you should see the page loaded in French, as shown in the following screenshot:

How it works...

We localized our application or website by doing two things. We first localized our templates so that we can have the static content translated into the correct language. We achieve this by using the built-in snippet called `Loc`. This snippet uses the string inside the tag—`welcome.text`, in our case—as a key and tries to find a resource in the bundle files defined by that key.

Lift has a built-in locale calculator that will try to find the correct bundle based on the language set in your browser, which is passed to the server via a parameter in the HTTP header request. For example, if the language set in your browser is German, Lift will try to find a `resources_de.properties` file. Three things can happen here:

▸ Lift finds the bundle file and renders the template in the correct language

▸ Lift doesn't find the file and then tries to find the default bundle—`resources.properties` in this case—and renders the text in the language set in the default bundle

▸ Lift doesn't find any bundles and then renders the template with `welcome.text` as the key—in our case

The same mechanism is applied to our `Localization` snippet and `MenuBuilder` snippet. When you use `S ? ("key")`, you are invoking the `?` method in the `S` object. This method will try to get the value defined by the key in a property file. The trick here is that the `?` method loads a localized string, which means that it will try to find a resource bundle file that best fits the locale defined in the request. How does Lift know which resource bundle file to use and where to find it?

Lift knows where to find the resource bundle file because we have already told it where they are when we added `LiftRules.resourceNames` in the `Boot` class, and it knows which file to use, because it uses the same resolution system used to find HTML templates—locale ISO codes.

In short, by calling the `?` method from the `S` object and using the built-in snippet called `Loc`, we localized the menu and the text loaded dynamically using resource bundles.

 This will not work when using localization with Comet actors because parameters in the HTTP request will be empty. In this case, it's better to keep localization information in `SessionVars`.

There's more...

The resolutions of both templates and bundle files follow the same logic. This means that Lift will try to find the template and bundle files starting in the most specific locale and moving toward the most generic one, as shown in the following example:

8. `baseName + "_" + language1 + "_" + country1 + "_" + variant1`

9. `baseName + "_" + language1 + "_" + country1`

10. `baseName + "_" + language1`

11. `baseName + "_" + language2 + "_" + country2 + "_" + variant2`

12. `baseName + "_" + language2 + "_" + country2`

13. `baseName + "_" + language2`

14. `baseName`

See also

- ▶ You can learn more about template localization at:

  - ❏ `http://simply.liftweb.net/index-8.1.html`

  - ❏ `http://exploring.liftweb.net/master/index-D.html`

  - ❏ `https://www.assembla.com/spaces/liftweb/wiki/ Internationalization`

- ▶ In addition, to learn more about resource bundles, visit: `http://docs. oracle.com/javase/6/docs/api/java/util/ResourceBundle. html#getBundle(java.lang.String,%20java.util.Locale,%20java. lang.ClassLoader)`

Testing snippets using Specs2

We cannot dilute the importance of testing software. The only way we can guarantee that our software works and will keep working after we have changed, refactored, and applied new features to it, is by testing it.

Getting ready

We'll use the code from the *Creating an HTML list using CSS selectors* recipe.

How to do it...

1. Create a file called `AnimalsSpec` in `src/test/scala/code/snippet` with the following content:

    ```scala
    import org.specs2.mutable._

    class AnimalsSpec extends Specification {
      "Animals list" should {
        "contains 5 animals" in {
          val result = <ul><li><span class="name">Dog</span> - <span
    class="sname">(Canis lupus familiaris)</span></li><li><span
    class="name">Cat</span> - <span class="sname">(Felis catus)</
    span></li><li><span class="name">Giraffe</span> - <span
    class="sname">(Giraffa camelopardalis)</span></li><li><span
    class="name">Lion</span> - <span class="sname">(Panthera
    leo)</span></li><li><span class="name">Horse</span> - <span
    class="sname">(Equus ferus caballus)</span></li></ul>
    ```

```
        val nodeSeq = Animals.list(<ul><li><span class="name"></
span> - <span class="sname"></span></li></ul>)

        nodeSeq.toString must ==/(result)
      }
    }
  }
```

2. Run the test in the SBT session by running the following command:

   `~test`

   You should see SBT executing the test and printing the result, as displayed in the following screenshot:

```
[info] AnimalsSpec
[info]
[info] Animals list should
[info] + contains 5 animals
[info]
[info]
[info] Total for specification AnimalsSpec
[info] Finished in 19 ms
[info] 1 example, 0 failure, 0 error
[info]
[info] Passed: : Total 1, Failed 0, Errors 0, Passed 1, Skipped 0
```

How it works...

Specs2 is a framework to create executable specifications. Each specification in Specs2 has the following format:

```
"Specification description" should
  "example one" in
  "another example" in
```

The first line defines `Fragment`, which is a trait defined by the Specs2 framework. What's happening here, is that Specs2 uses the string before the `should` method as `description`, and the string just after the opening of the `should` method as `Fragment`. The `Fragment` instance is, in this case, a set of examples that are constructed by the `in` method. Each block defined by the `in` method will be a test that will run during the execution of the tests.

An example will have one `description`, the string before the `in` method, and a body, which is the block between the curly braces. So, when the test runs, Specs2 executes the code defined in the body of every example and prints the description of the example with a green plus sign in case of success. If the execution fails, Specs2 prints a yellow X followed by the text **fail test**; it also prints the reason why the test failed. The printing will be different for cases when the example is skipped, pending, or erroneous.

Getting back to our test, we have created a specification for the `Animals` snippet, which contains one example that invokes the `list` method of the `Animals` snippet. The `list` method takes a `NodeSeq` object as a parameter and returns another `NodeSeq` object. Since we know what the output should be, we can compare the output produced by the method invocation with a fragment of HTML code. And that's all that the test is doing.

The `result` variable is the output we are expecting, and it will be compared with the output produced by the `list` method, stored in `NodeSeq val`.

Now that we have both fragments—the expected HTML and the HTML returned by the snippet—we can compare both of them using the DSL defined by the Specs2 framework. To compare both fragments, we invoked the `must` method, which takes a matcher as its parameter. The matcher is the code before and after the `must` method. The `==/` matcher compares two XML literals, and in this case, it will compare the values of the `NodeSeq` and `result` variables; if the values match, it returns `Success`.

There's more...

As you can see, testing snippets is just like unit testing any Scala code. And that makes testing snippets quite easy. But sometimes, the snippets might depend on HTTP variables and sessions. For such cases, you can mock an HTTP request using MockWeb or WebSpec.

For example, if you try to test a snippet that uses the `S.?` method and don't mock an HTTP request, you'll get the following error:

Cause: java.lang.IllegalStateException: Attempted to use resource bundles outside of an initialized S scope. S only usable when initialized

In such cases, you'll need to do something like this:

```
val expectedResult = MockWeb.testS("/someUrl") {
  // do something that requires having the context of an HTTP
    request or
  // such as using session variable and returns a value that can
    be
  // tested.
  1
}
```

What happens in this case is that the `testS` method sets up the required context for accessing `/somePath` as if you accessed the URL via a browser. So, you'll have access to `session` and `request` variables, for example.

Since testing snippets is just like unit testing Scala code, you can use any framework you want, such as JUnit, TestNG, and ScalaTest.

- ▸ To learn more about Specs2 and ScalaTest, please access the following addresses:
  - ❑ `http://www.scalatest.org/`
  - ❑ `http://etorreborre.github.com/specs2/`
- ▸ To learn more about mocking HTTP requests, please visit:
  - ❑ `https://www.assembla.com/spaces/liftweb/wiki/Mocking_HTTP_Requests`

Creating custom error pages

Even if we do test the applications we build, there are aspects and situations that we can't control—the user may type the wrong URL, we could have a problem with the network, or something that we didn't predict may happen and cause the application to fail.

That is why it is important to have a way to create pages to inform the user that something went wrong. Fortunately, Lift allows you to configure error pages based on HTTP response status codes.

Getting ready

You will need to perform the following steps before you begin creating custom error pages:

1. Create a new project.
2. Create a file called `404.html` by duplicating the `index.html` file.
3. Replace the content of the `div` tag with `main` as the value of `id` with the following code:

```
<h2>Error: 404</h2>
<p>Page not found!</p>
```

4. Create a new file called `403.html` by duplicating the `404.html` file.
5. Replace the content of `div` with `main` as the value of `id` with the following code:

```
<h2>Error: 403</h2>
<p>You don't have permission!</p>
```

6. Create a new file called `500.html` by duplicating the `404.html` file.
7. Replace the content of the `div` tag with `main` as the value of `id` with the following code:

```
<h2>Error: 500</h2>
<p>Something went wrong!</p>
```

8. We will add a dispatcher, which is a partial function whose pattern matches the request and executes a function of type `() => Box[LiftResponse]`, to simulate errors 500 and 403 by adding the following code into the `Boot.scala` file:

```
LiftRules.dispatch.append {
  case Req("error-500" :: Nil, _, _) => {
    () => {
      Full(InternalServerErrorResponse())
    }
  }
  case Req("error-403" :: Nil, _, _) => {
    () => {
      Full(ForbiddenResponse())
    }
  }
}
```

How to do it...

1. You first need to add the following menu items in the `Boot.scala` file:

```
Menu(Loc("403", "403" :: Nil, "403", Hidden)),
Menu(Loc("404", "404" :: Nil, "404", Hidden)),
Menu(Loc("500", "500" :: Nil, "500", Hidden)),
```

2. Then, you need to add response redirects for each custom error. You do this by adding the following code in the `Boot.scala` file:

```
LiftRules.responseTransformers.append {
  case r if r.toResponse.code == 403 =>
    RedirectResponse("/403")
  case r if r.toResponse.code == 404 =>
    RedirectResponse("/404")
  case r if r.toResponse.code == 500 =>
    RedirectResponse("/500")
  case r => r
}.
```

3. Start the application and access `http://localhost:8080/dont-exist`; you will see a page similar to that shown in the following screenshot:

app

Error: 404

Home

Static Content

Page not found!

Lift is Copyright 2007-2012 WorldWide Conferencing, LLC. Distributed under an Apache 2.0 License.

4. If you access `http://localhost:8080/error-500`, you will see the error 500 page, as shown in the following screenshot:

5. If you access `http://localhost:8080/error-403`, you will see the error 403 page, as shown in the following screenshot:

app

Error: 403

You don't have permission!

Lift is Copyright 2007-2012 WorldWide Conferencing, LLC. Distributed under an Apache 2.0 License.

How it works...

We achieved the goal of having custom error pages by creating a function that takes a `LiftResponse` value as its argument and returns `LiftResponse`, and appends it to `reponseTransformers`.

Our function pattern matches the `LiftResponse` value and checks its status code. If the response has an error status code—403, 403, or 500—the function returns a redirect response whose purpose is to redirect the user to the correct customized error page. But, if none of the error codes match, our function just returns the same `LiftResponse` value that was passed as parameter.

Since we are redirecting the user to a customized page, based on the HTTP status code, we need to create menu entries for these pages. This is necessary because if there are no entries in the SiteMap for these pages, Lift will return a 404 error, and since there is no 404 status code defined in the menu, we'll enter an infinity loop.

I have also defined a custom dispatcher to automatically return `ForbiddenReponse` and `InternalServerErrorResponse` if the user tries to access the `/error-403` or `/error-500` URL, because I wanted to show you what would happen in case of your application returning such responses due to an error or business logic that prevents the user from accessing some resources.

The downside to this approach is that the original error code is swallowed by Lift. This is because, when the response hits the `responseTransforms` rule, we just do a redirect. This means that you'll get a 302 code for the first path and then a 200 code for the custom error page.

In other words, if you access `/error-403`, you'll get response code 302 and then the 403 page will be loaded with response code 200.

There's more...

You can also fine-tune the error handling to catch exceptions and treat them accordingly. Let's say you want to redirect the user to a different page when a `SQLException` exception occurs.

To do this you would add the following code to the `Boot.scala` file:

```
LiftRules.exceptionHandler.prepend {
  case(_, Req(_, _, _), SQLException) =>
  RedirectResponse("/someCustomErrorPage")
}
```

What we are doing here is prepending to the exception handler a function that matches any URL for any type of request—GET, POST, and so on—in case of a `SQLException` exception and redirects the user to `/someCustomErrorPage`.

The first underscore (_) means that this rule will be applied to all run modes, such as production, development, test, and so on. You can change it to match only one run mode, if you want, by changing(_)for a string with the corresponding run mode—`production`—to match the production run mode.

The second underscore (_) is the URL that will have the exception handler. You can say that this exception handler will be attached to every URL in your application by using the underscore (_) character. However, you can define a specific URL by changing the underscore (_) character for the URL you want to attach the exception handler to, that is, `some :: path :: Nil`.

 In Lift, paths are usually represented as a list of strings. So this list, `some :: path :: Nil`, represents `/somepath`.

The fourth underscore (_) is the placeholder for the request type, such as `GetRequest` and `PostRequest`.

Sending JavaScript commands from the server

Sometimes there is a need to call a JavaScript function—to update the UI or for some other reason—depending on the result of some business logic that runs in the server.

If you are not using Ajax, the only way to achieve this is by redirecting the user to add a parameter in the URL, so you can check for its existence and decide whether to call the given function or not. For example, let's say that you need to execute a JavaScript function depending on the parameter `foo`. If you are not using Ajax, you'll have to redirect the user to `/somePage?foo=valueOfFoo`, and depending on the value of `foo`, decide whether your application should execute the JavaScript function or not.

Fortunately, Lift gives us a practical and easy way to accomplish this without the need to redirect the user, and this is what we will learn how to do in this recipe.

Getting ready

Perform the following steps before you start sending JavaScript commands from the server:

1. Create a new project.

2. Add the following code inside the `div` tag with `main` as the value of `id` in the `index.html` file:

```
<script>
  var myFunction = function() {
    $("#cmd1").html("function to show how to send js
      commands from the server.");
  }
</script>
```

3. Then, just after the `script` tag, add the following code:

```
<h2>Sending a js command from the server</h2>
<p>
  <span id="cmd1"></span>
  <hr />
  <span id="cmd2"></span>
  <hr />
  <span id="cmd3"></span>
  <script data-lift="JsCommand.jsCommand"></script>
</p>
```

How to do it...

1. Add the following code inside the `div` tag with `main` as the value of `id` in the `index.html` file:

```
<script>
  var myFunction = function() {
    $("#cmd1").html("function to show how to send js
      commands from the server.");
  }
</script>
```

2. Then, just after the `script` tag, add the following code:

```
<h2>Sending a js command from the server</h2>
<p>
  <span id="cmd1"></span>
  <hr />
  <span id="cmd2"></span>
  <hr />
  <span id="cmd3"></span>
  <script data-lift="JsCommand.jsCommand"></script>
</p>
```

3. Now, in the `snippet` package, create a file called `JsCommand.scala` with the following code:

```
import net.liftweb.util.BindHelpers._
import net.liftweb.http.js.JsCmds.{JsCrVar, Script}
import net.liftweb.http.js.JE.{JsFunc, JsRaw}
import net.liftweb.http.js.JsCmds
import xml.Text

object JsCommand {
  def jsCommand = {
    val command1 = JsCrVar("fromServer",
      JsRaw("""$("#cmd2").html("this string was sent from
        the server")"""))
    val command2 = JsFunc("myFunction").cmd
    val command3 = JsCmds.SetHtml("cmd3", Text("changing
      element content using Lift's JsCmds"))

    "*" #> Script(command1 & command2 & command3)
  }
}
```

4. Start the application and access `http://localhost:8080`. You should see a page similar to that shown in the following screenshot:

How it works...

The HTML we have created has nothing new in terms of concept or techniques. It's a regular HTML file with a JavaScript function, `myFunction`, which when invoked adds some text into the tag with `cmd1` as the value of `id`, and also invokes the `JsCommand` snippet.

The `JsCommand` snippet is also a regular snippet, in the sense that it defines a function that takes `NodeSeq` as a parameter and it returns a new, modified `NodeSeq` value. The difference lies in the fact that we are modifying the `span` tag for a `script` tag. We do this with the bind `"*" #> Script(...)`.

As you can see, we are passing `command1`, `command2`, and `command3` to the `Script` object. But, the `Script` object takes a `JsCmd` object as its argument. So, how are we passing three different things to it? As it turns out, the `&` character is a method—defined in the `JsCmd` trait—that takes a `JsCmd` object and returns a new `JsCmd` object. This new object contains the original object plus the one that was passed as argument. It is as if we are appending two `JsCmd` objects and creating a new one that contains both of them.

The object returned by the & method is a special kind of the JsCmd object called CmdPair. The following diagram is a UML diagram showing the hierarchy between JsCmd and CmdPair:

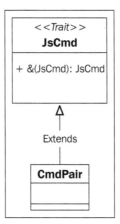

So, what is happening here is that command1 & command2 produces a CmdPair object, which we use to call its & method, passing command3 as the argument of the & method to create a new CmdPair object that will be passed to the Script object. In other words, we are concatenating JsCmd objects by using the & method. Let's take a look at each one of the commands to find out what they do.

The command1 variable uses the JsCrVar method, which takes a string and the JsExp object (JavaScript expression), and creates a variable named with the value of the string passed as its first parameter; this variable's content is the JavaScript expression passed as the second parameter to the JsCrVar method.

The result of JsCrVar("fromServer", JsRaw("""$("#cmd2").html("this string was sent from the server")""")) will be:

```
var fromServer = $("#cmd2").html("this string was sent from the
    server");
```

When this variable is evaluated, it changes the content of the span tag with cmd2 as the value of id, as you can see in the HTML that was rendered.

Also, note that we are using jQuery in the string passed as parameter for the constructor of the JsRaw class, and that's all it takes to create a JavaScript code that will be executed in the client. That's because the default template offered by Lift includes the path to jQuery. If you look at the default.html file in the templates-hidden folder, you'll find the following script tag:

```
<script id="jquery" src="/classpath/jquery.js"
    type="text/javascript"></script>
```

However, this only works because we are using `lift-jquery-module`, which provides jQuery for us.

 If you don't want to use jQuery or want to use a different version from the one provided by `lift-jquery-module`, just remove it from the `build.sbt` file and remove the script that loads jQuery from the template, or make the necessary changes to load the version you want to use.

The `command2` variable uses the `JsFunc` class, which takes two parameters and produces a call to a given JavaScript function. The first parameter is the name of the function that will be called, and the second, which is optional, is a list of parameters that will be used as arguments when calling the function. Let's say we do something like this:

```
JsFunc("someFunc", JsExp.strToJsExp("someValue")
```

This will produce the following output:

```
someFunc("someValue");
```

Since we are passing just one parameter—the name of the function—the output in the HTML will be:

```
myFunction();
```

When the HTML is loaded by the browser, it will call the function that we've created in the `myFunction` HTML file, causing the content of the `span` tag with `cmd1` as the value of `id` to be changed.

In the case of the `command3` variable, we used the `SetHtml` case class. It takes two arguments; the first is the ID of the element that will be changed and the second is the content that will be added into the element defined by the first argument. So, when we run `JsCmds.SetHtml("cmd3", Text("changing element content using Lift's JsCmds"))`, we are asking Lift to create a JavaScript code to change the content of the `span` tag with `cmd3` as the value of `id` by adding this text: changing element content using Lift's JsCmds.

The result of using the `SetHtml` class is the following JavaScript code, as you can see in the source of the HTML rendered:

```
jQuery('#'+"cmd3").html("changing element content using   Lift\u0027s
JsCmds");
```

There's more...

The `JsCmds` object has many more classes that make it capable of sending several JavaScript commands. For example, you can use the `JsCmds.Alert` class to invoke the JavaScript alert:

1. Add the following code in the `JsCommand` snippet we've created:

   ```
   val command4 = JsCmds.Alert("Alert sent from Lift").
   ```

2. Change the bind from `"*" #> Script(command1 & command2 & command3)` to `"*" #> Script(command1 & command2 & command3 & command4).`

3. Restart the application and access `http://localhost:8080`, and you should see an alert as shown in the following screenshot:

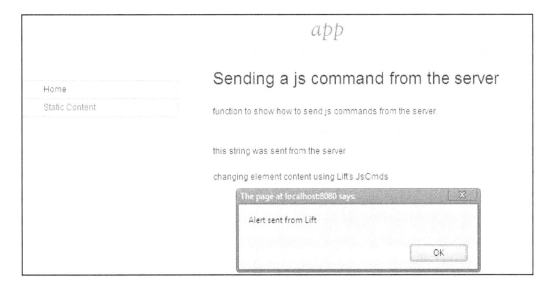

Similar to what happened when we used the `SetHtml` class, using the alert will make Lift render a call to the JavaScript alert in the HTML. If you take a look at the HTML source, you'll find the following code:

```
alert("Alert sent from Lift");
```

You can, create `for` loops using the `JsFor` and `JsForIn` classes, `if` statements using the `JsIf` object, and so on. It is worth spending some time playing with them. Or, if you prefer, you can create JavaScript code as strings and then call them in the HTML.

1. Add the following code in the `index.html` file:

   ```
   <div id="cmd4"></div>
   ```

2. Then, in the `JsCommand.scala` file, create a new method called `confirm`, with the following code:

```
def confirm = {
  val numbers = (1 to 10).toList
  val jsFunc =
  """
  var numbers = [""" + numbers.mkString(",") + """];
  for (i = 1; i <= """ + numbers.size + """; i++) {
    $("#cmd4").append('<button data-number="' + i + '">' +
    i + '</button>');
  }

  $("#cmd4 button").click(function() {
    confirm('Do you really want to delete number: ' +
      $(this).data("number"));
  });
  """.stripMargin

  JsRaw(jsFunc).cmd
}
```

3. Modify the `jsCommand` method by adding a new variable called `command5`:

```
val command5 = confirm
```

4. And then append the `command5` variable after the `command4` variable, as shown in the following code:

```
"*" #> Script(command1 & command2 & command3 & command4 &
command5)
```

5. Start the application and access `http://localhost:8080`; you will see 10 buttons, and when you click on any of them, you'll see a confirmation dialog as shown in the following screenshot:

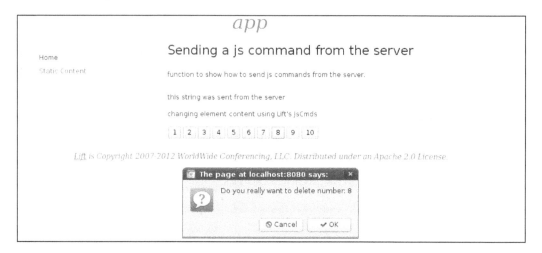

As explained earlier, what we did here is create JavaScript code using Scala's `jsFunc` variable, which is a string. But we added a little bit of complexity by creating a dynamic string to show how to create a dynamic JavaScript to be rendered on the page.

As you can see, Lift offers an abstraction layer over JavaScript that can be used to integrate server-side code with client-side code, and this abstraction is very powerful and flexible.

See also

▶   You can find more about Lift and JavaScript integration at `http://exploring.liftweb.net/master/index-10.html`

Invoking server-side functions from the client

In the previous recipe, we learned how to create JavaScript functions/code on the server and how to invoke/trigger those codes from the client. This is very useful, however, it's not enough, since there are times when we need to do the opposite. In other words, what do we do when we need to call a function on the server side using JavaScript? The solution is to use Ajax. In this recipe, we'll learn how to use Ajax and Lift's JavaScript abstraction layer to create a function on the server side and call it from the client side.

Getting ready

First of all, we will edit the `index.html` file.

1.   Invoke the snippet that will create the Ajax function that we are going to call, using the following code snippet:

```
<span class="lift:JsCommand.jsFunction"></span>
```

2.   Add a combobox containing some names and a button, as shown in the following code:

```
<div>
  <select id="person">
    <option value="Carly">Carly</option>
    <option value="Joe">Joe</option>
    <option value="John">John</option>
    <option value="Mary">Mary</option>
  </select>

  <button>Delete Selected</button>
</div>
```

3. After adding the combobox and the button, add the following JavaScript to call the Ajax function created by Lift when the user clicks on the button:

```
<script>
  $(document).ready(function() {
    $("button").click(function () {
      ajaxDeletePeople($("#person").val());
    });
  });
</script>
```

How to do it...

1. Create a file called JsCommand.scala in the snippet package, with the following content:

```
package code.snippet

import net.liftweb.util.BindHelpers._
import net.liftweb.http.js.JsCmds
import net.liftweb.http.js.JsCmds._
import net.liftweb.http.js.JE.JsRaw
import net.liftweb.http.SHtml
import net.liftweb.json._

class JsCommand {
  implicit val formats = net.liftweb.json.DefaultFormats

  var persons = "Carly" :: "Joe" :: "John" :: "Mary" :: Nil

  def loadData = {
    def funcBody(json: JValue) = {
      val p = json.extract[String]

      persons = persons.filterNot(_ == p)

      JsRaw(
        """
        $("#person [value='""" + p + """']").remove()
        """).cmd &
      JsCmds.Alert(p + " was removed")
    }
```

```
      Function("ajaxDeletePeople", List("personperson"),
        SHtml.jsonCall(JsRaw("person"), (value: Jvalue) =>
          funcBody(value)))
    }

    def jsFunction = {
      "*" #> Script(loadData)
    }
  }
```

2. Start the application and access `http://localhost:8080`; you should see a page
   similar to the following screenshot:

If you select a name in the combobox and click on the **Delete Selected** button,
you'll see an alert saying that the name you selected was deleted (see the following
screenshot); you will also see that the name is no longer in the combobox.

How it works...

As we've seen before, `<span class="lift:JsCommand.jsFunction"></span>` invokes
the `jsFunction` method in the `JsCommand` snippet. The `jsFunction` method transforms
the `script` tag due to the binding `"*" #> Script(loadData)`. So far, so good. We've
seen this in the previous recipe, and there is nothing new here. The good stuff is happening in
the `loadData` method that is passed as a parameter to the `Script` object.

The `loadData` method is composed of two blocks of code: an inner method called `funcBody` and a call to the `Function` object. The `Function` object creates a JavaScript function and takes three parameters—the function name, the list of parameters, and the function body.

When we say `Function("ajaxDeletePeople", List("person"), SHtml.jsonCall(JsRaw("person"), funcBody _))`, we are creating a JavaScript function called `ajaxDeletePeople`, which takes one parameter—`person`—and are creating a `GUIDJsExp` object as its body using the `Shtml.jsonCall` method and the parameter's second element.

The first parameter of the `jsonCall` method is the JavaScript expression that will be used to calculate the value to be sent to the server. In this case, we are saying that the value will be held by the variable `person`. The second parameter is the invocation of the `funcBody` function, passing whatever comes from the client as parameter.

If you take a look at the source of the HTML that was created in the browser, you will see the following code:

```
<script type="text/javascript">
  // <![CDATA[
  function ajaxDeletePeople(person) {
    liftAjax.lift_ajaxHandler('F428923197995KXSU5A=' +
      encodeURIComponent(JSON.stringify(person)), null, null,
      null);
  }

  // ]]>
</script>
```

The `ajaxDeletePeople` function was created by the `Function` object, `Function("ajaxDeletePeople"...` and the body of this function was created by the `Shtml.jsonCall` method. You can see that Lift creates an invocation to the `lift_ajaxHandler` method and passes a string composed by the GUID and the encoded JSON value represented by the `person` variable.

So, when `ajaxDeletePeople` is called, it calls the `lift_ajaxHandler` function, which will trigger a call—an HTTP request—to the server passing the GUID and the JSON object.

Lift gets the GUID and discovers which function it has to call. In our case, it is the `funcBody` method. Lift then calls the `funcBody` method, passing the JSON object as parameter. The `funcBody` method extracts the value of the JSON object using the method extract of the `JValue` class and stores it in the variable `p`. We use the value of the `p` variable to filter the list of names defined by the `persons` variable and return a new list that doesn't contain the value of `p`. This new list is then reassigned to the variable `persons`.

 Note that we could do something more complex here, such as deleting a record from the database or any other logic that could be necessary.

After removing the value from the list to simulate the deletion of some data, we create a JsCmd code, using the `JsRaw` class, to remove the value from the combobox. Also, we've created an alert to show which value from the combobox was removed.

`CmdPair` is composed by the jQuery code that removes the select option from the combobox, and the alert is the return value of the `funcBody` method.

Basically, we have created a way to tell Lift to create a JavaScript function that triggers an Ajax call to the server. This invokes the `funcBody` function that deletes data from the server and returns JavaScript commands that will update the UI.

The missing part is about how we bind the UI to this process. Well, the bind was created by the following JavaScript code that we added in the `index.html` file:

```
$("button").click(function () {
  ajaxDeletePeople($("#person").val());
});
```

This code triggers the `click` event of the `button` tag to invoke the `ajaxDeletePeople` function. The code is created on the server side, and it passes the value of the selected option as parameter to the `ajaxDeletePeople` function.

See also

> ▶ You can find out more about Lift and JavaScript integration at `http://exploring.liftweb.net/master/index-10.html`

3
Working with Forms

In this chapter, we will cover:

- ► Creating forms
- ► Validating forms
- ► Creating an Ajax form
- ► Creating multipage forms
- ► Defining a relationship between form fields

Introduction

What many UI-based applications have in common, is that they need a way to let the user input data. So, collecting data from the user is a feature that most applications should have. But in a web environment, how do we collect data?

The basic method is via forms. In this chapter, we will learn how to create forms—single page, multipage, and Ajax forms. We will also learn how to validate the data submitted by the user, how to wire form fields to create relations between them, and so on.

In other words, we will learn how to get and handle data submitted by the user in different ways.

Creating forms

In this recipe, we'll learn the basic technique for creating forms. Lift offers a neat and easy mechanism to help the creation of forms, called LiftScreen.

Getting ready

We'll modify the code that we used in the recipe, *Sending e-mails using Gmail's SMTP server,* in *Chapter 1, Getting Started with Lift Basics.*

You can duplicate and rename the code that we created before to keep the original example, or you can modify it during this recipe.

How to do it...

1. Replace the p tag and its contents in the index.html file with the following code:

    ```
    <div class="lift:SinglePageForm"></div>
    ```

2. Create a file called SinglePageForm.scala in the snippet package; it should contain the following code:

    ```
    package code.snippet

    import net.liftweb.http._
    import code.lib.SendEmail

    class SinglePageForm extends LiftScreen {
      val from = field("E-mail", "", "placeholder" ->
        "Enter your e-mail")
      val subject = field("Subject", "", "placeholder" ->
        "Enter the subject of your message")
      val body = field("Message", "", "placeholder" ->
        "Enter your message")

      protected def finish() {
        S.notice("form submitted")

        SendEmail.send_!(
          from,
          "to_email@example.com",
          subject,
          body
        )
      }
    }
    ```

3. You should see a form when you start the application and access `http://localhost:8080`, as shown in the following screenshot:

app

Welcome to your project!

Home
Static Content

E-mail	Enter your e-mail
Subject	Enter the subject of your r
Message	Enter your message

Cancel   Finish

Lift is Copyright 2007-2012 WorldWide Conferencing, LLC. Distributed under an Apache 2.0 License.

How it works...

As you can see, there is nothing new in the HTML file, except for the fact that we didn't add the method that should be invoked in the snippet. We are invoking the snippet called `SinglePageForm`, and that's it. Before getting into why we are invoking only the `SinglePageForm` snippet without any methods—in other words, explicitly—we must take a look at the snippet itself.

The first thing we will notice in the snippet code is that it extends the trait `LiftScreen`. Secondly, the snippet has a few variable declarations, and thirdly, it has a method called `finish`.

The `field` method used in the variable declarations is a method defined in the `AbstractScreen` trait. It's actually a convenient way to create `Field` objects.

 We can use the `field` method of the `AbstractScreen` trait because the `LiftScreen` trait extends it.

Each `Field` object defines a form field and can have validation rules and attributes, such as ID, class, and name.

So, when we say `field("E-mail", "", "placeholder" -> "Enter your e-mail")`, we are creating a `Field` object whose label will be `E-mail` and whose initial value will be an empty string; it will also have the `placeholder` attribute with the value `Enter your e-mail`. We have defined the `subject` and `body` fields in the same way. These field objects are text fields by default. That's why we see three textfields—`E-mail`, `Subject`, and `Message`—rendered on the page.

Now, we know how to define form fields using the `LiftScreen` trait, but we don't know how the **Cancel** and **Finish** buttons were added onto the page and how the submit process works.

Let's take a look at the `LiftScreen` trait and discover why we don't need to explicitly specify which method will be invoked in the `SinglePageForm` snippet. This will help us to find out how the **Cancel** and **Finish** buttons are rendered and also how the form is submitted.

`LiftScreen` provides a default dispatch method that is invoked when rendering the page. Then it calls the `toForm` method, which invokes a method called `renderHtml`. This last method is the one that will actually transform our field definitions into `NodeSeq`, which will be rendered in the browser. However, it does not only transform our definitions into `NodeSeq`; it also adds the **Cancel** and **Finish** buttons by invoking the `cancelButton` and `finishButton` methods respectively. Both methods take no argument and return an `Elem` class; this means that you can override both methods and customize them. For example, you can change the **Finish** button to **Save** by doing this:

```
override def finishButton = <button>Save<button>
```

The `renderHtml` method then binds the **Finish** button to the `finish` method, which is defined in our snippet. How does it know that we implement the `finish` method, so that it can be bound to the **Finish** button? The `finish` method is an abstract method defined in the `LiftScreen` trait, forcing us to implement the `finish` method in our snippet.

The `finish` method that we have implemented does two things. Firstly, it sends a message that will be displayed on the page, stating that the form was submitted, using the `notice` method of the `S` object. Secondly, it uses the `SendEmail.send_!` method to send the e-mail.

Note, that we are passing the fields that we've defined as parameters to the `send_!` method. However, it expects strings, not fields, so how does this work?

As it turns out, there is a `toString` method that is implicitly called in this case; this method returns an empty string or the value that the field holds.

There's more...

It is worth mentioning that it's possible to override both, the `toForm` method of `Field` objects, and the default template used by Lift, `wizard-all.html`, so you can have more control over how the page and the fields will be rendered in the browser.

See also

▶ You can find more information and examples on LiftScreen at: `https://www.assembla.com/spaces/liftweb/wiki/LiftScreen`

▶ To get more information about Lift messages, please visit: `https://www.assembla.com/spaces/liftweb/wiki/Lift_Notices_and_Auto_Fadeout`

Validating forms

In the previous recipe, we learned how to create a form so that users can submit data to the server. However, we didn't validate the data, and thus, it allows users to submit anything including invalid data, such as an invalid e-mail address or date.

The reason to validate data submitted by users is not only to prevent the application crashing from being fed data in an invalid format—for example, sending an email to an invalid e-mail address—but also for security reasons.

Getting ready

We are going to improve the code from the previous recipe by adding validation to the form we've created. You can duplicate the project to keep the previous section's code unmodified or you can modify it.

How to do it...

Carry out the following steps to validate the form:

1. In the `SinglePageForm.scala` file, add the following import statement:

   ```
   import java.util.regex.Pattern
   ```

2. Add the following line in the `SinglePageForm` snippet:

   ```
   val emailRegex = Pattern.compile("\\b[a-zA-Z0-9._%-]+
     @[a-zA-Z0-9.-]+\\.[a-zA-Z]{2,4}\\b")
   ```

3. In the `from` field declaration, add the following rule:

   ```
   valRegex(emailRegex, "Invalid e-mail")
   ```

4. Add the following rules in the `subject` field declaration:

   ```
       valMinLen(10, "Subject too short"),
       valMaxLen(140, "Subject too long")
   ```

5. For the `body` field, add these rules:

   ```
       valMinLen(20, "Message too short"),
       valMaxLen(400, "Message too long")
   ```

6. Remove the following `div` tag from the `default.html` file to prevent message duplication.

   ```
   <div class="lift:Msgs?showAll=true"></div>
   ```

7. Start the application and access `http://localhost:8080`.

If you submit the form without filling it in first, you will see some error messages on the page, as shown in the following screenshot:

How it works...

The difference between this code and the code from the previous recipe is that we have added a few validation helpers—valRegex, valMinLen, and valMaxLen—from the LiftScreen trait.

Each helper takes two arguments. The first argument is the value that will be used to check the user input, and the second argument is a string representing the message that will be displayed to the user in case the value entered by the user is not valid.

Through this quick explanation, the meaning of the helpers we've used becomes clear. The valRegex validation helper takes, as its first argument, a regular expression—in this case represented by the value emailRegex—and a message that tells the user that the e-mail entered is not valid. The valMinLen validation helper takes an integer as its first argument and validates the minimum length of the string entered by the user. On the contrary, valMaxLen takes an integer to define the maximum length that the string entered by the user can be.

In practical terms, what are we doing here is telling Lift not to allow users to enter invalid e-mail addresses, not to allow e-mail subjects shorter than 10 characters or longer than 140 characters, and not to allow e-mail body messages shorter than 20 characters or longer than 200 characters.

But how does Lift apply these rules? How do they work? Well, if you take a look at the source code of `LiftScreen`, you'll be able to see that every validation helper has the same structure:

```
protected def <helperName>(<base value>, <message>): <return> =
  <field value> match {
    case <success> => Nil
    case <failure> => List<FieldError>
  }
```

As you can see, each rule matches the field value against the control value, so the rule returns `Nil` in case of success, and as a `List<FieldError>` object in case of failure. So, let's take a look at how Lift would validate input using the rules we've set in our code. For example, we've set the rule `valMinLen(10, "Subject too short")`, for the `subject` field.

So, you can see that, in the preceding helper structure:

- `<helperName>` is `valMinLen`
- `<base value>` is `10`
- `<message>` is `"Subject too short"`
- `<return>` is a function that receives the value from the field `String =>` `List[FieldError]`
- `<field value>` is the value of the field
- `<success>` is a statement that checks the condition that should be checked
- `<failure>` is just a place holder

By changing the values from the code of the helper structure and what was stated in the previous paragraph, we'll have the following code:

```
protected def valMinLen(10, "Subject too short"):
  String => Lift[FieldError] = s =>
  s match {
    case str if str != null&& str.length > 10 => Nil
    case _ => List(FieldError(subject, "Message too short"))
  }
```

This real implementation of `valMinLen` is more abstract and has a few differences, but this example is pretty close to it.

`FieldError` is a class that holds the reference to the field that has the error and the message to be displayed on the page. So, if more than one field has errors, the `FieldError` object list will have more than one element. This means that for each field with invalid data, there will be a `FieldError` object in the `FieldError` object list.

We still need to see how Lift calls this rule to validate the form. Do you remember when I said that Lift calls the finish method when the user clicks on the **Finish** button? Well, what happens inside this method is that before calling the finish method that is defined in our snippet, it will call the validate method of the AbstractScreen trait. The LiftScreen trait mixes in the AbstractScreen trait. This method gets every field declared in the snippet and calls their validate method, which will trigger the execution of the rules we've defined for each field. After executing the validate method of each field, the validate method of the AbstractScreen trait will return an empty list if every value entered by the user is correct, or it will return a list of FieldError in case of any failure.

Lift will then invoke the finish method defined by us if no errors are found, or it will call the renderHtml() method to re-render the form and display the error messages.

This is the process by which Lift validates the data entered by the users.

In step 6, I mentioned that keeping the div tag that invokes the Msg snippet would cause the error messages to be duplicated. This is because the Msg snippet usually renders only generic messages—the ones that are not associated with an ID—and when passing the parameter showAll (set to true), causes the Msg snippet to render every message, including the ones associated with an ID, which is the case of the messages from FieldError objects. In practice, this means that the message will be rendered near the field that didn't pass the test because it is associated with the ID of the field; the message will also be rendered in div with the showAll parameter set to true.

There's more...

We've learned how to use the built-in validation helpers offered by Lift to create the basic rules of form validation. However, it is almost certain that you'll need to define more complex rules to validate forms when building your application.

Fortunately, we can create custom helpers and add them to our field definitions. Suppose we want the e-mail body to have at least three words, we will carry out the following steps:

1. Add the following code in the SinglePageForm snippet:

```
def minNumOfWords(num: => Int, msg: => String):
  String => List[FieldError] =
  s => s match {
    case str if (str != null) && str.split(" ").size >=
      num => Nil
    case _ => List(FieldError(currentField.box openOr new
      FieldIdentifier {}, Text(msg)))
  }
```

This method takes two parameters: the minimum number of words the e-mail body should have, and the message to be displayed in case the user enters a message with less than the minimum number of words.

2. Add the following code in the definition of the body field:

```
minNumOfWords(3,
    "The e-mail body should have at least three words")
```

By doing this, we are adding the custom rule that we have created into the e-mail body message, making Lift also apply this rule when validating the data.

After adding this custom validation rule, if you try to submit the form and do not enter at least three words in the message field, you will see the message, **The e-mail body should have at least three words**, as shown in the following screenshot:

Creating an Ajax form

We have seen how to create forms and validate them using Lift, and that is really neat. However, your application still has to reload the entire page to submit the forms and get a response from the server.

Things don't have to be this way! Lift is very flexible and provides a mechanism to add Ajax support into forms. In other words, we can build Ajax forms easily and thus not have to reload the whole page just to submit a form. In this recipe, we will learn how to create a form and submit it using Ajax.

Getting ready

We are going to change the form we built in the *Creating forms* recipe from a regular form to an Ajax form.

How to do it...

You can create an Ajax form by performing the following steps:

1. Remove the `div` tag that invokes the `SinglePageForm` snippet:

```
<div class="lift:SinglePageForm"></div>
```

2. And add the following code in its place:

```
<form class="lift:form.ajax">
    <div class="lift:AjaxForm.form">
        <div>
            <label for="from">From:</label>
            <input type="text" id="from">
        </div>
        <div>
            <label for="subject">Subject:</label>
            <input type="text" id="subject">
        </div>
        <div>
            <label for="message">Message:</label>
            <textarea id="message" cols="10"
                rows="8"></textarea>
        </div>
        <div>
            <input type="submit" value="Submit">
        </div>
    </div>
</form>
```

3. Then create a file called `AjaxForm.scala` in the snippet package and add the following code into it:

```
package code.snippet

import net.liftweb._
import http._
import js.JsCmds
import util.BindHelpers._
import code.lib.SendEmail

class AjaxForm {
  def form = {
    var from = ""
    var subject = ""
    var message = ""

    def process() = {
      SendEmail.send_!(
        from,
        "to_email@example.com",
```

```
          subject,
          message
        )

      JsCmds.Alert("Message sent") &
        JsCmds.SetValById("from", "") &
        JsCmds.SetValById("subject", "") &
        JsCmds.SetValById("message", "")
    }

      "#from" #> SHtml.text(from, from = _, "id" -> "from")
        &
        "#subject" #> (SHtml.text(subject, subject = _,
          "id" -> "subject")) &
        "#message" #> (SHtml.textarea(message, message = _,
          "id" -> "message") ++ SHtml.hidden(process))
    }
  }
```

4. Start the application and access `http://localhost:8080` in your browser.

    A form will be shown on the page, and you will see an alert saying that the message was sent when you hit the **Submit** button. This is shown in the following screenshot:

When you close the alert message, the form will be cleaned up.

How it works...

The `AjaxForm` snippet that we have created has one method called `form`, which is the method invoked in the HTML. This method binds the input fields in the HTML and replaces them with input fields that are created by the calls of the `SHtml.text` and `SHtml.textarea` methods.

The `SHtml` object is a Lift built-in object that makes the task of working with forms and Ajax easier because it offers a variety of methods, such as form fields and Ajax calls, to easily generate markup. For example, when you use `SHtml.text`, Lift allows you to generate the HTML code to create an input `text` field; likewise, if you use `SHtml.textarea`, Lift will create a `textarea` field. Both methods—`text` and `textarea`—take three parameters. The first one is the variable that holds the value that will be shown in the field. The second is a function called `Any`, which takes a string as an argument and can return anything. The third is an `ElemAttr` object list; in other words, a list of `attr-value` pairs that will be applied to the element. So, when we say `"#from" #> SHtml.text(from, from = _, "id" -> "from")`, we are binding the tag with `from` as the value of the `id` field in the HTML to the result of the invocation of the `SHtml.text` method, meaning that we'll replace the tag with `from` as value of the `id` field with the HTML code generated by the `SHtml.text` method.

Looking closely at the binding, we can see that we are using a variable called `from`, which was defined at the beginning of the `from` method as an empty string, and the first argument of the `text` method; that's why the field is empty when we load the page.

For the second argument, we are declaring an anonymous function that takes a string as its only argument and returns nothing: `(String) => Unit`. This function gets the string that was passed to it and assigns it to the `from` variable—`from = _`. The string that is passed is the one containing the value entered into the form by the user. In other words, we've created a function that takes the value from the form and assigns it to the `from` variable.

As the third argument states, we passed the `id-from` pair, meaning that the input text field that will be created by Lift will have the attribute `id` with value `from`. The same is true for both the subject text field and the message `textarea`. And this concludes the explanation on how to create form fields using Lift's API. However, it doesn't explain how the form is submitted.

Well, you can see that after invoking the `SHtml.textarea` method, we append—by invoking the `++` method—the call to the `SHtml.hidden` method, passing the `process` method as its argument. As you can imagine, this will create a hidden field bound to the `process` method.

If you take a look at the HTML source code generated, you'll see something like the following line of code:

```
<input type="hidden" name="F525418990340V1BAXG" value="true">.
```

The name of the input `hidden` field is the value generated by Lift to bind the field to the `process` method. So when the form is submitted, Lift knows what has to be executed.

Alright, now we know how all of the binds are done. When the `process` method is invoked, the variables that will be used as parameters in the invocation of the `SendEmail.send_!` method have the correct value because the anonymous function that we defined when invoking the `SHtml.text` and `SHtml.textarea` methods was called, it assigned the values from the form to the variables.

After sending the e-mail, by invoking the `SendEmail.send_!` method, the `process` method does two more things. Firstly, it sends a JavaScript command to display an alert, and secondly, it cleans the form field up by setting the field values to empty strings by creating the `SetValById` classes. This class takes two arguments: the first one is the ID of the element that will get the new value, and the second is the value itself.

We've seen how the form is created and how it is processed, but we still don't know how it is submitted.

As you can see in the `index.html` file, we are invoking two snippets. One of them is the snippet we've created—`AjaxForm`—and we know how it works; the other is a Lift built-in snippet called `Form`: `<form class="lift:form.ajax">`

When you invoke the `Form` snippet, Lift will wrap your snippet into its own snippet. In other words, Lift will create a `form` tag around the HTML generated by your snippet. We can check this by looking at the HTML source generated in the browser. This is what you'll find:

```
<form id="F2506649547422RDOLZ" action="javascript://"
  onsubmit="liftAjax.lift_ajaxHandler(jQuery
  ('#'+&quot;F2506649547422RDOLZ&quot;).serialize(),
  null, null, &quot;javascript&quot;);return false;">
```

As you can see, Lift has created a `form` tag and it also added an `onsubmit` attribute to it, which is an Ajax handler. When the user clicks the submit button, it triggers the Ajax handler defined in the `onsubmit` attribute, which will trigger an Ajax call to the server, thus submitting the form. Once the server gets the call, it will trigger the functions defined by the second arguments passed to the methods that create the fields, and when it starts processing the `hidden` field, it will invoke the `process` method and the e-mail will be sent, the alert will be shown, and the form will have its field values reset.

There's more...

We can validate Ajax forms by creating a few rules and check them before sending the e-mail:

1. First remove the following code from the `default.html` file and add it just before the `div` tag containing the `from` field in the `index.html` file:

   ```
   <div class="lift:Msgs?showAll=true"></div>
   ```

2. Then, add the following code into the `process` method in the `AjaxForm` snippet:

```
if (!emailRegex.matcher(from).matches()) {
  S.warning("From is not a valid e-mail")
  Noop
} else if (subject.trim.length < 10 ||
  subject.trim.length > 140) {
    S.warning("Subject should have at least 10 chars and
      have no more than 140.")
    Noop
} else if (message.trim.length < 20 ||
  message.trim.length > 400) {
    S.warning("Message should have at least 20 chars and
      have no more than 400.")
    Noop
} else {
    <previous code from process method>
}
```

It you try to submit the form without filling it in correctly, you will see an error message before the **From** field as shown in the following screenshot:

Now, when the form is submitted and the `process` method is invoked, it validates the values of the variables—`from`, `subject`, and `message`—and if anything fails, it sends a message to the client and returns an empty JavaScript command, `Noop`. And if everything goes fine, it sends the e-mail and resets the values of the form fields.

The message is created by the invocation of the `S.warning` method and is displayed in the client by the invocation of the `Msgs` snippet.

Creating multipage forms

Sometimes a single page form is all that you need to get your job done, but there are times when we need more. In such situations, we need an easy way to deal with multipage forms; this means that we need a way to keep the values between the pages, a way to validate all fields, pages and so on, and a way to change the flow of the form based on how the user filled in some fields.

Lift provides a powerful and flexible tool to accomplish this. It is called `Wizard`.

Getting ready

In this section, we will learn how to create a multipage form using `Wizard`. We will start with preparing our application to be able to use `Wizard`.

1. Create a new project.

2. Add `lift-wizard` as a dependency by adding the following line into `libraryDependencies ++= Seq` in the `build.sbt` file:

    ```
    "net.liftweb"        %% "lift-wizard"        % liftVersion
      % "compile"
    ```

3. Add the following code into the `div` tag with `main` as the value of the `id` field in the `index.html` file:

    ```
    <div class="lift:MultiPageForm"></div>
    ```

4. Create a file called `finish.html` in the `webapp` folder. It should be identical to the `index.html` file except for the fact that we'll change the `div` tag, replacing the invocation to the `MultiPageForm` snippet with an invocation to the `Msgs` snippet:

    ```
    <div class="lift:Msgs?showAll=true"></div>
    ```

How to do it...

1. Edit the `Boot.scala` file and add a new entry into the `entries` value to serve the finish page:

    ```
    Menu.i("Finish") / "finish"
    ```

2. Create a new snippet called `MultiPageForm` in the snippet package, containing the following code:

```scala
package code.snippet

import net.liftweb._
import http._
import js.JsCmds.RedirectTo
import wizard._

object MultiPageForm extends Wizard {
  val userData = new Screen {
    val name = field("Name", "")
    val email = field("E-mail", "")
  }

  val addressData = new Screen {
    val line1 = field("Address line 1", "")
    val line2 = field("Address line 2", "")
    val line3 = field("Address line 3", "")
    val city = field("City", "")
    val state = field("State", "")
    val zipCode = field("Zip code", "")
  }

  def finish() {
    val name = userData.name.is
    val email = userData.email.is
    val line1 = addressData.line1.is
    val line2 = addressData.line2.is
    val line3 = addressData.line3.is
    val city = addressData.city.is
    val state = addressData.state.is
    val zip = addressData.zipCode.is

    S.redirectTo("/finish",
      () => {
        S.notice("Name: " + name)
        S.notice("E-mail: " + email)
        S.notice("Address Line 1: " + line1)
        S.notice("Address Line 2: " + line2)
        S.notice("Address Line 3: " + line3)
        S.notice("City: " + city)
        S.notice("State: " + state)
        S.notice("Zip Code: " + zip)
      }
    )
  }
}
```

3. Start the application and access `http://localhost:8080`. You should see a page containing two fields—**Name** and **E-mail**—and two buttons—**Cancel** and **Next**. This is shown in the following screenshot:

If you click on the **Next** button, you will see the second page of the form, as shown in the following screenshot:

After filling in both pages of the form and clicking the finish button, you'll see a page containing a list with the values that you entered in the form, as shown in the following screenshot:

How it works...

We won't take too much time explaining how both of the HTML files work because they are simple snippet invocations. The `index.html` file invokes the `MultiPageForm` snippet and the `finish.html` file invokes the `Msgs` snippet.

The first thing you should notice in the `MultiPageForm` snippet is that it extends the `Wizard` trait. This trait holds a list of `Screen` objects. `Screen` is actually a trait that extends the `AbstractScreen` trait. This is the same trait used by `LiftScreen`. As you can imagine, everything that we learned about the `LiftScreen` trait and how to build a form using it is true when dealing with `Screen` objects.

You can see that we are creating two `Screen` objects in here—the `userData` and `addressData` variables:

```
val userData = new Screen …
val addressData = new Screen …
```

You can also see that the `Screen` object has values that are fields; they are the same ones we used to create the form fields for the single page form. The `userData` object of `Screen` has two fields—`name` and `email`—and the `addressData` object of `Screen` has six fields—`line1`, `line2`, `line3`, `city`, `state`, and `zipCode`.

You can think of each screen of the form as being a single page form, and that Lift does all of the plumbing to put the pages together in a way that it can be seen by the user as a single form that has more than one page. What Lift does to achieve this trick, is to keep track of the field values when navigating through the form. So, when the user fills in the first page and clicks on **Next**, Lift stores the values in a `RequestVar` object, which is a variable that holds its value during the lifetime of the page being rendered, and renders the next page; this goes on until the user reaches the last page and clicks on the **Finish** button. When this happens, Lift invokes the `finish` method—just like it did with the single page form—so we also need to implement it here.

You can see that we are doing two things in the `finish` method. We are assigning the values of each form field to a new variable, and then we are redirecting the application to the **Finish** page. The redirect is necessary if the next page that you'll show to the user is not a form. That's because, once the `finish` method is done, the `Wizard` trait will reset the form and will send that application back to the first page. So, if we just do the invocations to `S.notice`, we'll see the messages rendered above the fields on the first page of the form. To make sure the redirect works, we need to add a new entry in the `SiteMap` to serve the `/finish` path.

Reassignment of the values is necessary because we won't have access to the form variables after the redirect. So, for example, if you try to say `S.notice("Name: " + userData.name.is)`, you'll see just the text **Name:**, on the **Finish** page, and no value in front of it.

There's more...

I've said that `Wizard` is a list of `Screen` objects and that each `Screen` object works as a single page form, `LiftScreen`, because both extend the `AbstractScreen` trait. To prove this point, we'll use the validations we added to the form in the *Validating forms* recipe in this chapter, and as you can imagine, it will work just like it did before.

1. Add the following code just before the definition of the `userData` variable in the `MultiPageForm` snippet:

    ```
    val emailRegex = Pattern.compile
      ("\\b[a-zA-Z0-9._%-]+@[a-zA-Z0-9.-]+\\.[a-zA-Z]{2,4}\\b")
    ```

2. Modify the `userData` definition by adding the `valMaxLen` and `valMinLen` validations in the `name` variable:

    ```
    valMinLen(10, "Name too short"),
    valMaxLen(140, "Name too long")
    ```

3. Add the `valRegex` validation into the e-mail address:

    ```
    valRegex(emailRegex, "Invalid e-mail")
    ```

Now, if you start the application and try to submit the form without correctly filling it in, you'll see messages stating that you didn't add the proper values to the fields. This is shown in the following screenshot:

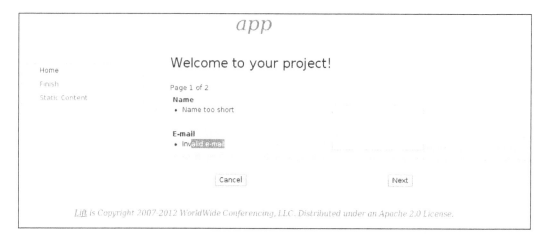

Another neat thing we can do is to modify the form flow. To do this, we'll add a new `Screen` object into our form, making it have three screens.

1. So, create a new `Screen` object called `paymentData` containing the following code:

    ```
    val paymentData = new Screen {
      val creditCardName = field("Credit card name", "")
      val creditCardNumber = field("Credit card number", "")
      val creditCardExpDate = field
        ("Credit card expiration date", "")
    }
    ```

2. Add the variables to hold the values of the new fields inside the `finish` method:

    ```
    val ccName = paymentData.creditCardName.is
    val ccNumber = paymentData.creditCardNumber.is
    val ccExpDate = paymentData.creditCardExpDate.is
    ```

3. And add the notices for the newly created fields so that they can be shown on the **Finish** page:

    ```
    S.notice("Credit card name: " + ccName)
    S.notice("Credit card number: " + ccNumber)
    S.notice("Credit card expiration date" + ccExpDate)
    ```

Right now, we have a form with three pages which goes from pages one, to two, to three in a straight flow. But that's not what we want.

1. On the `userData` object of `Screen`, create a new field, which will be a checkbox. Lift automatically creates a checkbox field if you pass a Boolean value to the `field` method, as shown in the following code:

```
val hasAddress = field("I already have an address",
    false)
```

2. While still in `userData`, override the method `nextScreen` with the following code:

```
override def nextScreen = if (!hasAddress)
    addressData else paymentData
```

What's new in this example, is that we've overridden the definition of the `nextScreen` method. This is the method invoked by Lift to determine which page it should show next. As you can see, we've changed the original flow of the form from page one, to page two, to page three by placing a conditional statement. So, if the user marks the checkbox, the `hasAddress` value will be `true`, making the execution enter the `else` part, thus making the `nextScreen` method return the `paymentData` object of Screen. If the user doesn't mark the checkbox, the `nextScreen` method will return `addressData`.

See also

▸ The *Creating forms* recipe in this chapter
▸ The *Validating forms* recipe in this chapter

Defining a relation between form fields

Another neat feature that Lift provides is Cells, which like cells in a spreadsheet can be wired together, so when the value of one cell changes, it automatically updates the value of another one.

In this recipe, I'll mix Ajax forms with Cells to teach you how to create a dynamic shopping cart. Thus, when the user updates the quantity of a given item he or she wants to purchase, the total amount per item and the total shopping cart amount will be updated.

Getting ready

You can use the code from the examples we've used in the previous recipes, or you can start a new project.

Modify the `index.html` file by removing everything inside the `div` tag, with main as the value of the `id` field, and add the following code into it:

```
<div data-lift=" ShoppingCart.show">
    <table>
        <thead>
        <tr>
            <th>Item</th>
            <th>Quantity</th>
            <th>Price</th>
            <th>Total</th>
        </tr>
        </thead>
        <tbody>
        <tr>
            <td class="item"></td>
            <td class="quantity"></td>
            <td class="price"></td>
            <td class="total"></td>
        </tr>
        </tbody>
        <tfoot>
        <tr>
            <td colspan="3">Total</td>
            <td class="cart-total"></td>
        </tr>
        </tfoot>
    </table>
</div>
```

How to do it...

Follow these steps to create a relation between the form fields:

1. Create a snippet called `ShoppingCart` in the `snippet` package, with the following code:

```
package code.snippet

import net.liftweb.util.{DynamicCell, ValueCell}
import net.liftweb.util.BindHelpers._
import net.liftweb.http.{WiringUI, SHtml}
import net.liftweb.http.js.JsCmds
import net.liftweb.http.js.JsCmds._
```

```
case class Item(id: Int, name: String, qty: Int, prc: Double) {
  val quantity = ValueCell(qty)
  val price = ValueCell(prc)
  val total = quantity.lift(_ * price)
}

class ShoppingCart {
  val items = Item(1, "Item 1", 10, 1) ::
    Item(2, "Item 2", 1, 10) ::
    Item(3, "Item 3", 2, 1.5) ::
    Item(4, "Item 4", 3, 2.5) :: Nil

  val cartTotal = DynamicCell(() => items.foldLeft(0d)((acc, i) =>
acc + i.total.get))

  def setQuantity(i: Item, qty: Int, totalId: String) = {
    if (i.quantity.get < qty || i.quantity.get > qty) {
      i.quantity.set(qty)
      JsCmds.SetValById(totalId, i.total.get)
    } else {
      Noop
    }
  }

  def show = {
      "tbody *" #> {
        items.map(i => {
          val totalId = i.id.toString

          ".item *" #> i.name &
          ".quantity *" #> SHtml.ajaxText(
            i.quantity.get.toString,
            v => setQuantity(i, v.toInt, totalId)          ) &
          ".price *" #> WiringUI.asText(i.price.get) &
          ".total *" #> WiringUI.asText(i.total)
        })
      } &
      ".cart-total *" #> WiringUI.asText(cartTotal)
  }
}
```

2. Start the application and access `http://localhost:8080` in your browser; you should see a page which looks like a shopping cart, as shown in the following screenshot:

As you change the value of the fields in the **Quantity** column, the values in the **Total** column will be updated automatically.

How it works...

In the `index.html` file, we've invoked the method `show` of the `ShoppingCart` snippet and we have also created the table structure that will hold the items of the shopping cart, namely, item name, quantity, price, and total per item. It will also have the total value of the cart.

Let's start looking at the snippet to find out how the HTML code that we've put in the `index.html` file turns into a dynamic shopping cart.

Starting with the `show` method, we can see that there is a bind to the content of the `tbody` tag—`tbody *`—and a bind to the `td` tag with class `cart-total` of the `tfoot` section. The `tbody` bind creates a list of `CssSel` elements, one for each item in the shopping cart, which are represented by the elements in the `items` list.

A shopping cart item is represented by the case class `Item`. This class has an ID, a name, a quantity, a price, and a total value, which is the price multiplied by the quantity.

You will notice that we have used the `qty` and `prc` parameters to set the `quantity` and `price` attributes respectively and that these attributes belong to `ValueCell`. The `ValueCell` object is one of the three types of `Cell` objects that is provided by Lift and it also holds a value that can be mutated.

The attribute `total` is a `FuncCell` object of `Cell`, which holds a value that is created by applying a function to the value of another `Cell` object.

```
val total = quantity.lift(_ * price)
```

You can see in the preceding code, that we have created a `FuncCell` object of `Cell` by lifting the quantity into a function that multiplies the quantity by the price—`_ * price`—and have assigned it to the `total` attribute.

Now that we've seen how the `Item` class is defined, we can get back to the binds. As I was saying, the `tbody` bind creates a list of `CssSel` elements that are generated by the application of the function `(Item) => CssSel`, which is the argument of the `map` method—`items.map(...)`. This function binds the name of the item to the `td` tag where the `class` attribute equals `item`. It then creates a text field, which is bound to an Ajax handler, and it binds this text field to the `td` tag with `quantity` as the value of the `class` attribute. The Ajax handler will then invoke the method `setQuantity`; we'll soon see how this works.

And the last part of the `show` method creates a bind between the `asText` method of the `WiringUI` object and those `td` tags where `class` equals `price`, `total`, and `cart-total`. The only difference is the value that we are passing as parameter in each one of the bindings.

Right now, we know how the binds are done and how the HTML is generated, but we still don't know how the fields are updated automatically.

Let's start with the total of each item. Since we've told Lift that the value of the `total` cell is calculated by the application of a function to the value of the `quantity` cell, each time we set a new value in the `quantity` cell, the `total` cell is automatically updated.

The next piece of the puzzle is the `ajaxText` field that we've bound to the **Quantity** column in the table. Every time the user changes the value and takes the focus out of the field, an Ajax call is triggered; this will invoke the `setQuantity` method. This method does two things. It sets a new value in the `quantity` cell of the item and sends a JavaScript command to update the value of the **Total** field on the page if the quantity has changed. Alternatively, it does nothing if the user enters the same value in the quantity field.

You can see that we are passing the value of the `total` cell to the JavaScript command, and this works because when the `quantity` cell is updated, the `total` cell is updated too.

This is how we've used Cells and JavaScript to create a dynamic shopping cart.

There's more...

Ajax fields and JavaScript commands are not the only way to update the UI when working with Cells.

We can use the `WiringUI` object, which offers a practical way to render the UI on top of Cells and Wiring.

You can see an example of the use of `WiringUI` in the bind of the `td` tag with the class `total` in the table's `tfoot` section—`".cart-total *" #> WiringUI.asText(cartTotal)`. What we are doing here is creating a text node—the `span` tag—that will be rendered inside the `td` tag using the `cartTotal` variable as its argument. `cartTotal` is a `DynamicCell` type of `Cell`, which changes its value at each access. This means that every time a dependent `Cell` value changes, the value of `DynamicCell` is recalculated. You can see that we've created this `Cell` as being the sum of the values of the total `Cell` objects of each item in the cart; in other words, it is the sum of the total of each item. So, each time the total of any item changes, it triggers the recalculation of the `cartTotal` variable, which makes the `WiringUI.asText` method update the UI, and it's because of this mechanism that we can see the total value changing each time we update the value of the quantity fields.

I hope I've demonstrated to you how powerful and flexible Lift is by letting the limit of what we can do become the limit of our imagination. All we need to do is to put these pieces together in imaginative ways to build complex forms that offer an extraordinary user experience.

4

Working with REST

In this chapter, we will cover the following topics:

- ▶ Getting data from the server
- ▶ Creating data using the REST service
- ▶ Modifying data using the REST service
- ▶ Deleting data using the REST service
- ▶ Testing a REST service using Specs2
- ▶ Uploading a file using the REST service
- ▶ Creating an RSS feed

Introduction

In the early days of the Internet, the websites and applications were standalone as they had no means of communicating with each other. Each application was like an island that had to collect and store every piece of data it could possibly need to get the job done.

Today, almost everyone in the world connects to the Internet through notebooks, cell phones, or tablets. Therefore, applications should be able to communicate with each other so that users can access any information they need from their cell phones, notebooks, or any other device.

Each application that communicates with the external world must provide an **API** (**Application Programming Interface**) to specify how the applications will interact. However, having an API is not enough. We still need HTTP to transport the data.

How did the need for building APIs and using HTTP as the transportation layer lead to REST?

REST, which stands for **Representational State Transfer**, is a style or pattern for creating consistent APIs. Thus, the application will have a uniform interface to send and retrieve representations of states of resources, which are meaningful concepts such as a user, an order, and so on. Another advantage of a REST API is that it simplifies and decouples the server and client sides. As a result, REST is becoming the most common option chosen to export application features to external resources when creating APIs.

In this chapter, we will learn how to build an application to create and maintain data about clients—CRUD operations—using a REST interface to serve as the communication bridge between the server and the client.

 CRUD stands for Create, Retrieve, Update, and Delete.

Our REST API will be composed of the following URLs:

Method	URL	Action
GET	/clients	Retrieves the list of clients
GET	/clients/<id>	Gets the data for the client with the specified ID
POST	/clients	Creates a new client
PUT	/clients/<id>	Modifies the client data with the given ID
DELETE	/clients/<id>	Deletes the client data with the given ID

Each section will handle one of the URLs mentioned in the preceding table. However, this is not the end of the story. We will learn how to upload files to the server and how to create an RSS feed using a REST API at the end of this chapter.

Getting data from the server

In this recipe, we will learn how to build URLs to respond to GET requests. In other words, we will learn how to serve data to the clients of your API. This means that you will be able to create a REST URL, where you can fetch a collection from data of a given resource—data about clients in this case—or fetch data about a specific resource.

Getting ready

You can either use example codes, which we have used in the recipes from previous chapters, or you can start a new project.

After creating the project, we will need to create a list of clients to serve as an in-memory database. We will need a model class to keep the data that will be shown on the page:

1. Inside the `code.model` package, let's create a class named `Client` with the following code:

```
package code.model

import net.liftweb.json.JsonDSL._

case class Client(id: Int, name: String, email: String) {
  def asJson = {
    ("id" -> id) ~
      ("name" -> name) ~
      ("email" -> email)
  }
}
```

2. Let's create a new package, named `session`, inside the `code` package. Then, create an object named `ClientCache` with the following code:

```
package code.session

import code.model.Client

object ClientCache {
  var clients: List[Client] = Nil

  def startClient() {
    if (clients.isEmpty)
      clients = (1 to 10).toList.map(i => Client(i, "Client " + i,
"client_" + i + "@email.com"))
  }
}
```

3. Invoke the method `startClient()` inside the `boot` method, which is in the `Boot` class, with the following code snippet:

```
ClientCache.startClient()
```

How to do it...

Now, carry out the following steps to see the list of clients:

1. Create a new package called `rest` inside the `code` package.

2. Now, create an object called `Clients` in it. This object should have the following code:

```
package code.rest

import net.liftweb.http.rest.RestHelper
import net.liftweb.http._
import net.liftweb.json.JsonDSL._
import net.liftweb.util.Helpers._
import code.session.ClientCache
import code.session.Clients
object Clients extends RestHelper {
  serve({
    case Req("api" :: "clients" :: Nil, _, GetRequest) =>
listClients()
  })

  def listClients() = JsonResponse ("clients" ->
ClientCache.clients.map(_.asJson))
}
```

3. Add the following line in the `boot` method of the `Boot` class to register our object as a dispatcher:

```
LiftRules. statelessDispatch.append(Clients)
```

4. Modify the `index.html` file by creating a table to hold the data inside the `div` tag with `main` as the value of `id`:

```
<table>
    <thead>
    <tr>
        <th>Id</th>
        <th>Name</th>
        <th>E-mail</th>
        <th>View</th>
        <th>Delete</th>
    </tr>
    </thead>
    <tbody>
    </tbody>
</table>
```

5. Now, create the JavaScript code to call the REST API and display the data in the web page, as shown in the following code:

```
<script type="text/javascript">
        $(document).ready(function() {
            $.ajax({
                url: "/api/clients",
                contentType: "application/json"
            }).done(function (data) {
```

```
            var clients = "";

            $.each(data.clients, function(i, client) {
                clients += '<tr>' +
                    '    <td>' + client.id + '</td>' +
                    '    <td><input type="text" value="' +
client.name + '"></td>' +
                    '    <td><input type="text" value="' +
client.email + '"></td>' +
                    '    <td>View</td>' +
                    '    <td>Delete</td>' +
                    '</tr>';
            });

            $("tbody").html(clients);
        });
    });
});
</script>
```

6. Start the application.

7. Access `http://localhost:8080`.

You should see a web page containing a list of clients in your browser:

app

Welcome to your project!

Home

Static Content

Id	Name	E-mail	View	Delete
1	Client 1	client_1@email.com	View	Delete
2	Client 2	client_2@email.com	View	Delete
3	Client 3	client_3@email.com	View	Delete
4	Client 4	client_4@email.com	View	Delete
5	Client 5	client_5@email.com	View	Delete
6	Client 6	client_6@email.com	View	Delete
7	Client 7	client_7@email.com	View	Delete
8	Client 8	client_8@email.com	View	Delete
9	Client 9	client_9@email.com	View	Delete
10	Client 10	client_10@email.com	View	Delete

How it works...

When working with REST, you need to create a dispatcher that tells Lift how to handle the requests sent to your REST API. The dispatcher is an object that extends the built-in `RestHelper` object, which defines some helper methods, such as the `serve` method, which adds request handlers to work with REST. One of the methods defined by the `RestHelper` object, which we used to define the endpoint, is the `serve` method. This method takes an argument as a partial function, which takes a `Req` object and returns a `LiftResponse`. In other words, we passed the `serve` method a pattern match block that associates request paths to methods that return HTTP responses.

In our case, we defined a match that handles requests—of type GET—sent to the path `/api/clients`, that calls the `listClients` method. The first parameter that we passed to the `Req` object is a list of strings that defines the path `/api/clients`. The second parameter defines the extension; for example, if you pass JSON as the second argument, the path will be `/api/clients.json`. Since we passed—underscore—as its second argument, it does not matter what the extension of the endpoint is. The third and last parameter of the `case` defines the type of HTTP request—GET, POST, PUT, or DELETE.

The `list` method gets the clients from the `ClientCache` object and transforms it into a list of JSON objects by calling the `asJson` method, which is defined in the `Client` class. Let's see how this transformation works.

To transform a Scala object into a JSON object, we used the DSL `JsonDSL` defined by Lift. This DSL defines methods such as `->` and `~`, which help us tell Lift how the transformation should be done. For example, when you use the code snippet `("id" -> id) ~ ("name" -> name)`, the DSL will return the object `JObject( JField("id",JInt(id)) :: JField("name",JString(name)) :: Nil)`. As you can see, the DSL creates a `JObject`, which contains a list of `JField` objects. Each `JField` object, is composed by a name—`String`—and a value—`JValue`. If the variable being transformed is a `String`, it will be converted into a `JString` object; otherwise, if it is an `Int`, it will be converted into a `JInt` object.

Going back to the `asJson` method, you can see that it will take the current client instance and will return a `JObject` (which is also a `JValue`), containing three `JField` objects—one for the client's name, one for the e-mail, and the third one for its ID. We then get the list of JSON objects—`JObject`—and we pass it to the `JsonResponse` object.

The `JsonResponse` object gets the list of JSON objects and then builds a `LiftResponse`—which will be an HTTP response with the status code `200`—with the proper response headers, cookies, and our objects.

Now that we know how the API works on the server side, let's take a look at the client side.

In the `index.html` file, we used jQuery's Ajax feature to invoke our API; at the time of getting the response from the server, if it iterates the list of JSON objects and creates the HTML elements—table rows—then the HTML elements will be inserted into the table we've defined.

> The JavaScript code used is just an example to show how the REST API works, that is, how it handles a request and how it sends a response.

Now, the user will see the final result, which is the table containing one client per row, as you can see in the screenshot at the end of this recipe's *How to do it...* section.

There's more...

Now, let's learn how to fetch a specific client:

1. First, we need to add the new URL in our dispatcher by adding a new `case` statement into the `serve` method. Create the `serve` method in the `Clients` object using the following code snippet:

```
serve({
    case Req("api" :: "clients" :: AsInt(id) :: Nil, _,
GetRequest) => getClient(id)
    case Req("api" :: "clients" :: Nil, _, GetRequest) =>
listClients()
    })
```

2. Then, still inside the `Clients` object, you'll need to define the `get` method as follows:

```
def getClient (id: Int) = {
    val client = ClientCache.clients.filter(_.id == id).map(_.
asJson).headOption

    client match {
      case Some(c) => JsonResponse.apply(c)
      case _ => NotFoundResponse()
    }
}
```

3. Then, in the `index.html` file, find the following line:

```
'    <td>View</td>' +
```

and change it to:

```
'    <td><a href="#" class="view" data-id="' + client.id +
'" onclick="showDetail(this)">View</a></td>' +
```

4. Now, inside the `script` tag, create the `showDetail` function with the following code:

```
var showDetail = function(element) {
    $.ajax({
        url: "/api/clients/" + $(element).data("id"),
        contentType: "application/json"
    }).done(function (client) {
        $("#client-id span").html(client.id);
        $("#client-name span").html(client.name);
        $("#client-email span").html(client.email);
        $("#client-data").show();
    });
};
```

Restart the application, refresh the page, and click on one of the **View** links, and you should see a web page with a list of clients and a section at the top with the details of the client you clicked on, as shown in the following screenshot:

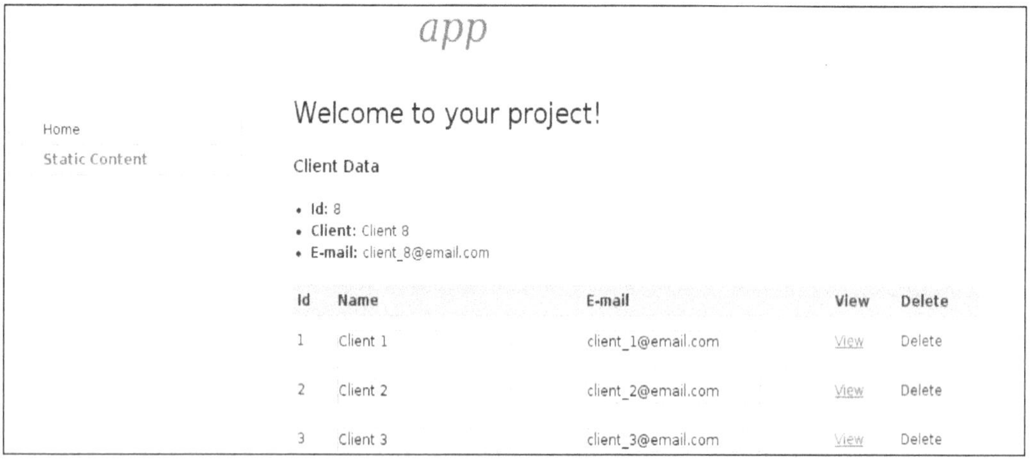

The mechanisms behind fetching a collection of objects from the server and a single one are very similar and we must learn what the differences are.

There are two important differences. The first is the endpoint; to fetch a collection of a given resource, we call `/api/clients`, while to fetch one resource only, we must call `/api/clients/<id>` (where `<id>` is the unique identifier of the resource). We have defined this new endpoint by creating the following new `case` entry in the `server` method:

```
case Req("api" :: "clients" :: AsInt(id) :: Nil, _, GetRequest) =>
getClient(id)
```

If you compare both `case` statements, you can see that they are identical and the only differences are:

▸ The new entry path has a new element: `AsInt(id)`

▸ The method that it calls is the `getClient` method

The new element of the path is a value—called `id`—that will be converted into an `Int` value by the `AsInt` object. This variable will be used as the parameter when invoking the `getClient` method. The `getClient` method filters the client list in the `ClientCache` object by their IDs and calls the `asJson` method to the client whose ID matches the ID passed to the `getClient` method. Then, it "pattern matches" the value it gets after filtering the client list and passes the JSON representation of the client to the `JsonResponse` object, thus returning a HTTP response with the status code `200`, and containing the client object as a JSON object. However, if the filter cannot find any client, the `getClient` method will return a `NotFoundResponse`—error code 404.

The last missing point is how the client side interacts with this endpoint. Well, you can see that we've created a link that invokes the `showDetail` function when the user clicks on it, as shown in the following snippet:

```
<td><a href="#" class="view" data-id="' + client.id + '"
onclick="showDetail(this)">View</a></td>' +
```

The `showDetail` function then triggers an Ajax call—a GET HTTP request—to the path we have defined. When the server responds, it gets the values from the JSON object that the server sent, adds them into the HTML, and then shows the `div` element with its ID `client-data`, which contains the values we retrieved from the server.

Now that we know how to fetch data from the server, we will learn how to create new data using a REST API.

Creating data using the REST service

Now that we know how to fetch data, the next step is to learn how to create the data so that we can fetch it later.

Thus, we will learn how to create the REST URL, which will respond to the POST request.

Getting ready

We are going to modify the code we created in the previous recipe. You can duplicate the project from the last recipe to keep it separated or you can use the same one.

1. Remove the following line from the `boot` method in the `Boot` class:

```
ClientCache.startClient()
```

2. Then modify the `ClientCache` object by adding a new `import` statement:

```
import net.liftweb.http.SessionVar
```

3. Remove the `clients` variable and the `startClient` method, and modify the object declaration from `object ClientCache` to `object ClientCache extends SessionVar[List[Client]](Nil)`.

4. At last, in the `index.html` file, create a form to input data using this code:

```html
<div>
    <form>
        <fieldset>
            <legend>New Client</legend>
            <div><label for="name">Name:</label><input
type="text" id="name"></div>
            <div><label for="email">Email:</label><input
type="text" id="email"></div>
            <div> <button>Submit</button> </div>
        </fieldset>
    </form>
</div>
```

5. Create a JavaScript function to send the data to the server, as follows:

```javascript
var createClient = function() {
var client = {
    name: $("#name").val(),
    email: $("#email").val()
};

$.ajax({
    async: false,
    type: "post",
    url: "/api/clients",
    data: JSON.stringify(client),
    contentType: "application/json"
}).done(function (data) {
    var newLine = '<tr>' +
                '   <td>' + data.id + '</td>' +
                '   <td><input type="text" value="' +
data.name + '"></td>' +
                '   <td><input type="text" value="' +
data.email + '"></td>' +
                '   <td><a href="#" class="view" data-
id="' + data.id + '" onclick="showDetail(this)">View</a></td>' +
                '   <td>Delete</td>' +
```

```
                          '</tr>';

                  $("tbody").append(newLine);
                  $("form")[0].reset();
              });
          };
```

6. We also need to bind the button's `onclick` event listener to call the `createClient` function:

```
              $("button").click(function() {
                  createClient();
              });
```

How to do it...

Carry out the following steps to input data:

1. Define a new URL inside the `serve` method:

```
case "api" :: "clients" :: Nil JsonPost json -> _ =>
createClient(json)
```

2. Create a `case` class that will represent the data we get from the request:

```
case class JClient(id: Option[Int], name: String, email: String)
```

3. Create a method to convert the data received in the request into a `Client` object:

```
implicit def jClient2Client(jClient: JClient): Client = {
    val nextId = ClientCache.is.size + 1

    Client(jClient.id.getOrElse(nextId), jClient.name, jClient.
email)
  }
```

4. Create the method that will save the new client data on the server with the following code snippet:

```
def createClient (json: JValue) = {
    val client: Client = json.extract[JClient]
    ClientCache.set(client :: ClientCache.is)

    JsonResponse (client.asJson)
  }
```

5. Start the application.

6. Access `http://localhost:8080`.

You will see that the web page now has a form where you can input data, as shown in the following screenshot:

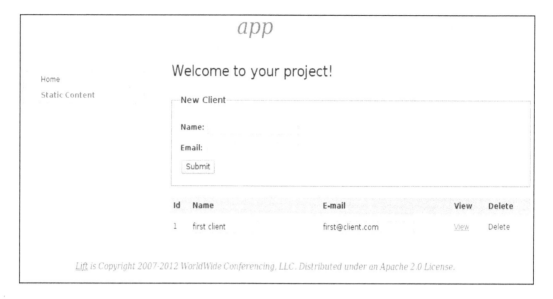

How it works...

The server-side part is simple; as you can see, it consists of a few lines of code. The first thing to notice is that we have created a new endpoint to respond to HTTP POST requests. However, there are many things going on.

Most of them have to do with the `JsonPost` value, which is defined as follows in the `RestHelper` trait:

```
protected lazy val JsonPost = new TestPost[JValue] with JsonTest
    with JsonBody
```

So, when the server gets the POST request, it tests the request to see whether it is a POST request with JSON data in its body and awaits a JSON response. If this is the case, it will extract the path, the JSON object, and the `req` object from the request.

The JSON object will then be assigned to the `json` value and the `req` object will be discarded due to the use of the _ character. We then pass the `json` value to the `createClient` method. But, we still need to extract the values out of the JSON object and create a new client object with it. We do this by invoking the `extract` method from the `JValue` object. This method can extract values from JSON objects using case classes. In our case class, we told the extract method to use the `case` class `JClient` to extract the values from the JSON object.

You can see that the `JClient` class is a representation of the JSON object, meaning that for each attribute that is present in the JSON object, it must be present in the `case` class.

Once we have extracted the values from the JSON object, we can add it to our list of clients. However, there is a small catch here; the list of clients, which is kept in the `ClientCache` object, is a list of `Client` objects not a list of `JClient` objects. So how is it possible to extract a `JClient` object from the JSON object and add it into the list of clients?

This is possible because we have defined an implicit conversion to convert `JClient` objects into `Client` objects. So, when we use this code `val client: Client = json.extract[JClient]`, the `extract` method will create a `JClient` object. Then, the implicit conversion will be invoked and will create the `Client` object, which will be assigned to the `client` value. We then prepend the client object to the client list, and then set this new list as the client list of the `ClientCache` object.

The last step is to return the newly added object to the client side with an HTTP response with the status code `200`, in order to tell the client that everything worked and that the client was successfully added. We do this by converting the object—`Client`—into a `JObject` and passing it, as a parameter, to the `JsonResponse` object. Let's see how the client side interacts with this endpoint.

First of all, we defined an HTML form—composed by two textfields and a submit button—so we can input the data that we want to use to create our clients.

We have also bound the button's `onclick` event listener to call the `createClient` function everytime the user clicks on it.

The `createClient` method creates a JSON object using the values entered into the form and triggers an Ajax call—HTTP POST Request—to the URL `/api/clients`, passing the JSON object in the request body. Once the server finishes its job—by adding the client into the `ClientCache` object—we do two things. Firstly, we create a new line in the list of clients using the data that came from the server, and secondly, we reset the form.

There's more...

We have modified the `ClientCache` object and changed it into a `SessionVar` object. But what is a `SessionVar` object anyway?

A `SessionVar` object is an object that basically has two features:

- It has a lifetime similar to the HTTP session attributes
- It is type safe

You can use a `SessionVar` object whenever you need to keep a value around for periods longer than a few HTTP requests.

You can learn more about implicit conversions in Scala by visiting the following URLs:

▶ `http://www.scala-lang.org/node/114`

▶ `http://www.artima.com/weblogs/viewpost.jsp?thread=179766`

Modifying data using the REST service

We now know how to build a REST API to fetch and create data, but what if our client has moved to a new office or changed their phone number?

We will need to have a way to modify our client's data and this is what we will learn in this recipe.

Getting ready

We will keep evolving the code that we have created in the last recipe. So, again, you can duplicate the last section's project or just modify it.

1. In the `index.html` file, create a new column in the table to hold the edit link:

    ```
    <th>Edit</th>
    ```

2. Create a new function called `createLine`, which should have the same code as the `createClient`'s `newLine` variable. This code is as follows :

    ```
    var createLine = function(data) {
        return <place the code from the newLine variable
    here>
    };
    ```

3. Then add the new column, by adding the following code:

    ```
                    '    <td><a href="#" class="edit" data-
    id="' + data.id + '"
    onclick="editClient(this)">Edit</a></td>' +
    ```

4. In the `createClient` function, change the following line:

    ```
    $("tbody").append(newLine);
    ```

    to:

    ```
    $("tbody").append(createLine(data));
    ```

5. Now, create a function called `editClient` with the following code:

```
var editClient = function(element) {
    var name = $(element).parents("tr").find(":input")[0];
    var email = $(element).parents("tr").find(":input")[1];

    var client = {
        id: $(element).data("id"),
        name: name.value,
        email: email.value
    };

    $.ajax({
        async: false,
        type: "put",
        url: "/api/clients/" + client.id,
        data: JSON.stringify(client),
        contentType: "application/json"
    }).done(function (data) {
        alert(JSON.stringify(data));
    });
};
```

6. Change the highlighted line that starts with `client +=` to `clients +=` `createLine(client);`, from the following code:

```
clients += '<tr>' +
             '   <td>' + client.id + '</td>' +
             '   <td><input type="text"
value="' + client.name + '"/></td>' +
             '   <td><input type="text"
value="' + client.email + '"/></td>' +
             '   <td><a href="#"
class="view" data-id="' + client.id + '"
onclick="showDetail(this)">View</a></td>' +
             '   <td>Delete</td>' +
             '</tr>';
```

How to do it...

Now, carry out the following steps:

1. Create the new URL in the `Clients` dispatcher by adding the following code into the `serve` method:

```
case "api" :: "clients" :: AsInt(id) :: Nil JsonPut
json -> _ => editClient(id, json)
```

2. Now, create the `editClient` method, which should have the following code:

```
def editClient(id: Int, json: JValue) = {
  val client: Client = json.extract[JClient]
  val newList = ClientCache.is.filter(_.id != id)

  ClientCache.set(client :: newList)

  JsonResponse (client.asJson)
}
```

3. Start the application.

4. Access `http://localhost:8080`.

Now, you will see a page similar to the one shown in the following screenshot:

How it works...

Once again, the server side is simple and straightforward. You will notice that we have used the same technique to create a new client, and we are going to use it again. However, instead of using the `JsonPost` value to extract a JSON object from a POST request, we have used the `JsonPut` value.

This means that when we send a PUT request to the URL `/api/clients/<id>`, Lift will extract the JSON object from the request's body and pass it with the ID extracted from the URL, to the `editClient` method. The `editClient` method will use the same implicit conversion to transform the `JClient` object that was extracted from the JSON object, into a `Client` object.

Now that we have the value sent from the browser stored in the client variable, we can edit the data. In this example, we are not actually editing the client, we are just removing the client with the same ID from the `ClientCache` object and adding a new one, which has different values but the same ID.

After updating the list of clients, the `editClient` method returns the modified client as a JSON object in the HTTP response, by converting the `Client` object into a `JObject` object and passing it to the `JsonResponse` object.

On the client side, we have to change a few things to integrate the UI with the API. First, we need to create a function to create the JSON object and send it to the server to edit the client data. To achieve this, we created the function called `editClient`, which gets the values from the input fields and creates a JSON object, and then stores it in the `client` variable.

After creating the JSON object, it fires an Ajax call to the endpoint we defined earlier. Once the server finishes the updating process and responds to the client, it captures the JSON object that the server sends back and shows it in an alert dialog. We have now created a new column in the client list to create a link that calls the `editClient` function.

Deleting data using the REST service

Our application to manage clients using a REST API is almost ready. The last thing that we need to learn is how to destroy data using our API.

Getting ready

As you can imagine, you have only two options. Either duplicate the project from the last section or keep evolving the same project.

1. In the `index.html` file, modify the `createLine` function by changing the line with the `Delete` column from:

```
'    <td>Delete</td>' +
```

to:

```
'        <td><a href="#" data-id="' + data.id + '"
onclick="deleteClient(this)">Delete</a></td>' +
```

2. Create the `deleteClient` function, which will make the delete call to the server:

```
var deleteClient = function(element) {
    $.ajax({
        async: false,
        type: "delete",
        url: "/api/clients/" + $(element).data("id"),
        contentType: "application/json"
    }).done(function (data) {
        $(element).parents("tr").hide();
    });
};
```

How to do it...

Now carry out the following steps:

1. First, modify the `serve` method in the `Clients` dispatcher by adding the following line:

```
case Req("api" :: "clients" :: AsInt(id) :: Nil, _,
DeleteRequest) => deleteClient(id)
```

2. Create a new method called `getById` in the `Clients` object, as shown in the following code:

```
def getById(id: Int) = ClientCache.is.find(_.id == id)
```

3. Modify the `geClient` method from:

```
def getClient(id: Int) = {
  val client = ClientCache.is.filter(_.id == id).map(_.asJson).
headOption

  client match {
    case Some(c) => JsonResponse.apply(c)
    case _ => NotFoundResponse()
  }
}
```

to:

```
def get(id: Int) = {
  getById(id) match {
    case Some(c) => JsonResponse (c.asJson)
    case _ => NotFoundResponse()
  }
}
```

4. Create a new method called `deleteClient` with the following code:

```
def deleteClient(id: Int) = {
    getById(id) match {
```

```
       case Some(c) => {
         val newList = ClientCache.is.filter(_.id != c.id)

         ClientCache.set(newList)

         JsonResponse (c.asJson)
       }
       case _ => NotFoundResponse()
     }
   }
```

5. Start the application.

6. Access `http://localhost:8080`.

You should see a web page containing a **Delete** link in each line, as shown in the following screenshot:

How it works...

To remove data from the server, we have used a technique similar to the one that we use to fetch a given client. This means that our API will delete data when it gets a DELETE HTTP request in this address: `/api/clients/<id>`. However, this is the same URL which we have used to fetch data from a single client to display in the browser. So, how does Lift know when we want to fetch or delete data?

It knows because of the HTTP request type that we have used in the `case` statements. To simply fetch data, we used a GetRequest, while to delete data, we used a DeleteRequest, which is a case object that defines DELETE as the HTTP method of the request.

Another thing to note, is that we have used the `AsInt` object to extract the client ID from the URL and pass it to the `deleteClient` method—just as we did earlier to fetch the data for a given client. The delete method filters the client list from the `ClientCache` object and creates a new list that does not contain the client that we want to delete, and stores this new list in the `ClientCache` object. Then, it returns the client that we have just removed from the list in the HTTP response, using the `JsonResponse` object. The `deleteClient` method also returns an HTTP response with error code 404 if it cannot find the client that we want to delete in the list of clients.

On the client side, we created a function named `deleteClient` to trigger the Ajax call to delete the client. You can see that the HTTP request of the Ajax call will have the type `delete`, which will match against the delete endpoint. This function hides the line containing the deleted client once it gets a response from the server.

Testing a REST service using Specs2

As the API is subject to change in the future, it will be nice if we could create automated tests which we can easily run to confirm that we aren't breaking anything when making such changes.

In this recipe, we'll learn how to test REST APIs using Specs2.

Getting ready

As in the previous recipes, you can duplicate the project you used earlier or you can keep modifying the same one by adding the following dependency in the `build.sbt` file:

```
"net.liftweb"        %% "lift-testkit"        % liftVersion
            % "test"
```

How to do it...

1. Now, create the specification named `ClientsSpec` in `src/test/scala/ code/ rest` using the following code:

```
package code.rest

import org.specs2.mutable.Specification
import net.liftweb.mockweb.MockWeb._
import code.model.Client
import code.session.ClientCache
import net.liftweb.http.JsonResponse
import net.liftweb.json.JsonDSL._
```

```
class ClientsSpec extends Specification {
  val clients = Client(1, "First", "first@test.com") ::
    Client(2, "Second", "first@test.com") :: Nil

  "Client REST API" should {
    "list clients" in {
      testS("/api/clients") {
        ClientCache.set(clients)

        val expectedResp = JsonResponse("clients" -> clients.
map(_.asJson))

        Clients.listClients() ==== expectedResp
      }
    }

    "fetch details from a given client" in {
      testS("/api/clients/1") {
        ClientCache.set(clients)

        val expectedResp = JsonResponse(
          clients.head.asJson,
          Nil, Nil,
          200
        )
        Clients.getClient(1) ==== expectedResp
      }
    }

    "be able to create new clients" in {
      testS("/api/clients") {
        val expectedResp = JsonResponse(
          clients.head.asJson,
          Nil, Nil,
          200
        )

        Clients.createClient(clients.head.asJson)
        Clients.getClient(1) ==== expectedResp
        ClientCache.is.size === 1
      }
    }
  }
}
```

You should see output similar to that in the following screenshot, after running the `test` command—which will make the tests run—inside the `sbt` session:

```
[info] ClientsSpec
[info]
[info] Client REST API should
[info] + list clients
[info] + fetch details from a given client
[info] + be able to create new clients
[info]
[info]
[info] Total for specification ClientsSpec
[info] Finished in 122 ms
[info] 3 examples, 0 failure, 0 error
```

How it works...

Testing REST services becomes simple when we bind the endpoint to a method. All we need to do is test the method itself. Since the method used by the endpoint is just a regular Scala method, we can unit test in it.

In this case, I chose to test them with the Specs2 framework, which we have already seen how it works in the recipe *Testing snippets using Specs2*, in *Chapter 2, Working with HTML*. However, there is a need to introduce `lift-testkit` to create and run the tests because the REST service we've built depends on the `SessionVar` object.

The problem with the `SessionVar` objects is that they are bound to an HTTP context, which means that to be able to make the tests to work, we'll need to mock HTTP requests, and this is exactly what `lift-testkit` provides.

You can see that we call the method `testS` inside each test. This method set up the `S` object, which represents the state of an HTTP request/response. The request that will be mocked uses the URL that is passed as the parameter to the `testS` method. So, in the first test, we'll mock a request to `/api/clients`. Now, inside the `testS` method, we are able to set any value we want in `ClientCache SessionVar`, which is the data source of our REST API. So, to actually test the list endpoint, we need to have some data that we can fetch. For this purpose, we've added two clients in the `ClientCache` object by using the `SessionVar.set` method—`ClientCache.set(clients)`. At this point, we have everything that we need to test ready, and what we have left to do is call the method that we want to test and compare the result.

This is what we did when we compared the result from the call of the `listClients` method with the `expectedResp` variable—which is what we expect the `listClients` method to return. The test will pass if the values on both sides of the`===` method match, and it will fail if they don't.

There's more...

To test the creation of a new client, we used the same technique. The difference is that we didn't set the `ClientCache` object upfront.

We first called the `createClient` method, and then we tested its content to check if it had the expected value—only one client.

See also

  ▸ See the *Testing snippets using Specs2* recipe in *Chapter 2, Working with HTML*

  ▸ To learn more about `lift-testkit`, visit:

     `https://www.assembla.com/spaces/liftweb/wiki/Mocking_HTTP_`
     `Requests`

Uploading a file using the REST service

We know now how to build a REST API that responds to the basic HTTP methods—GET, POST, PUT, and DELETE. However, we were dealing only with JSON data until now, but what if you also want to allow the users of your application to upload files?

In this recipe, we will learn how to send a file to the server and then save it in the local filesystem.

Getting ready

1. Create a new project or modify the one we used in the last section.

2. Edit the `index.html` file by adding the following form in the `div` element with `main` as the value of `id`:

```html
<form enctype="multipart/form-data" action="/api/files"
method="post">
            <fieldset>
                <legend>New File</legend>

                <div>
                    <label for="uploadFile">File:</label>
                    <input type="file" id="uploadFile"
                      name="uploadFile"/>
                </div>
                <div>
                    <input type="submit" value="Submit"/>
                </div>
            </fieldset>
        </form>
```

3. Add a new key named `file.folder` in the `default.props` file which is located in `src/main/resources/props/`, as shown in the following code:

```
file.folder=<someFolder>
```

4. Change `<someFolder>` to the folder where you want to save the file.

How to do it...

Now carry out the following steps in order to upload the file:

1. Create a new object named `Files` in the `code.rest` package under `src/main/scala/` with the following code:

```
package code.rest

import net.liftweb.http.rest.RestHelper
import net.liftweb.http._
import java.io.{File, FileOutputStream}
import net.liftweb.util.Props

object Files extends RestHelper {
  serve {
    case "api" :: "files" :: _ Post req => uploadFile(req)
  }

  def uploadFile(req: Req): LiftResponse = {
    req.uploadedFiles match {
      case FileParamHolder(_, mime, fileName, data) :: Nil => {
        val path = Props.get("file.folder", "") + "/" + fileName

        val fos = new FileOutputStream(new File(path))
        fos.write(data)
        fos.close()
      }
      case _ =>
    }

    RedirectResponse("/")
  }
}
```

2. Append the `Files` object to `LiftRules.dispatch` as:

```
LiftRules.dispatch.append(Files)
```

3. Start the application.

4. Access `http://localhost:8080`.

You will see a web page containing a form with only one field named **File**, as shown in the following screenshot:

If you submit the form, you will see that the file was saved in the folder you set in the `default.props` file earlier.

How it works...

First of all, we have defined a new endpoint so that we can upload the file. This new endpoint—`/api/files`—was bound to the `uploadFile` method.

This method invoked the `uploadedFiles` method from the `req` object, which returns a list of `FileParamHolder` objects. A `FileParamHolder` class holds the files uploaded via a multipart-data form.

Its attributes are as follows:

- The name of the form field
- The MIME type that was specified in the request's content type
- The name of the file
- The array of bytes that is the content of the file

In our case, since we are sending only one file, the `uploadedFiles` method will return a list containing only one `FileParamHolder` entry. We will then use the returned list in a pattern match to extract the file attributes and bytes. When we use `FileParamHolder(_, mime, fileName, data) :: Nil` in the `case` statement in the pattern match, it means that we want a list of a single element and that this element is a invoked `FileParamHolder`. We are also saying that we are only interested in the last three parameters that were used to construct the object. Inside the `case` statement, we will have the MIME type, the name of the file, and the array of bytes available.

You can see that we use the name of the file—the `fileName` variable—and the value we defined in the `default.props` file, to define the whole path where the file will be saved. Then, we use the `path` variable to create the `file` object and pass it to the `FileOutputStream` object.

Once you have the `FileOutputStream` object, you can invoke the `write` method and pass the array of bytes—the `data` variable—to write the content of the file.

After this step, the file is saved and we can close the `FileOutputStream` object and redirect the user to the home page.

Creating an RSS feed

In this recipe, we will learn how to use the techniques we have learned so far to build **RSS** (**Rich Site Summary**), which is a format to deliver content that changes regularly.

By providing an RSS feed for the content of your site, you will allow people to have a convenient way of staying informed by retrieving the latest content of your application. RSS feeds are convenient because people don't need to access each site that they want to read content from. All they need to do is add the RSS feed URL into their favorite newsreader and all of the content the person is interested in will be in one place.

Getting ready

One last time, you can duplicate the project you used in the previous recipe, or you can keep modifying the same one.

How to do it...

Carry out the following steps to create an RSS feed:

1. Create a new endpoint to serve the feed, using the following code in the `Clients` object:

   ```
   case Req("api" :: "clients" :: "feeds" :: "rss" :: _, _,
   GetRequest) => toRss(getClients)
   ```

2. Create an `implicit` method to transform XML objects into arrays of bytes:

   ```
   implicit def elemToByteArray(value: Elem): Array[Byte] = {
     value.toString().getBytes
   }
   ```

3. Create an object named `DateUtils` inside the package `lib` under `src/main/scala/code/` with the following code:

```
package code.lib

import java.text.SimpleDateFormat
import java.util.Date

object DateUtils {
  def formatDate(format: String)(date: Long): String = {
    val sdf: SimpleDateFormat = new SimpleDateFormat(format)
    sdf.format(new Date(date))
  }

  def longDate(date: Long): String = formatDate("yyyy-MM-
dd'T'HH:mm:ssZ")(date)
}
```

4. Create the method `getClients` to build the XML that will be served, as follows:

```
def getClients: Elem = {
  <rss version="2.0">
    <channel>
      <title>Clients</title>
      <description>List of clients by RSS feed</description>
      <link>http://localhost:8080/api/clients/feeds/rss</link>
      <lastBuildDate>{longDate(Calendar.getInstance().
getTimeInMillis)}</lastBuildDate>
      <pubDate> {longDate(Calendar.getInstance().
getTimeInMillis)} </pubDate>
      {ClientCache.clients.flatMap {
        c =>
          <item>
            <title>Client: {c.id}</title>
            <description>Name: {c.name} - E-mail: {c.email}</
description>
            <pubDate> {longDate(Calendar.getInstance().
getTimeInMillis)} </pubDate>
          </item>
        }}
    </channel>
  </rss>
}
```

5. Create the method to build the response that will be sent to the client:

```
def toRss(elem: Elem): LiftResponse = {
  InMemoryResponse(
    elem,
    ("Content-Type" -> "application/rss+xml") :: Nil,
    Nil,
    200)
}
```

6. Start the application.

7. Access `http://localhost:8080/api/clients/feeds/rss`.

Now, you will see the following RSS feed:

Clients

List of clients by RSS feed

Client: 1
04/12/2013 08:06 PM

Name: Client 1 - E-mail: client_1@email.com

Client: 2
04/12/2013 08:06 PM

Name: Client 2 - E-mail: client_2@email.com

Client: 3
04/12/2013 08:06 PM

Name: Client 3 - E-mail: client_3@email.com

How it works...

You can see that we have created a new endpoint to serve the RSS feed, and bound this endpoint to the method `toRss` in the previous section.

This method takes an `Elem` object as its argument and returns an `InMemoryResponse`. This means that it will take the `Elem` object and push it directly into the `Response` object. The conversion from an `Elem` object into an array of bytes is done by the `implicit` method `toByteArray`. Since we've defined this method as implicit, we can pass the `Elem` object directly to the `InMemoryResponse` class, which takes an `Array[Byte]` as it's first parameter.

The second parameter of the `InMemoryResponse` class is a list of HTTP headers that we used to define the content type of the response as being `application/rss+xml`.

> `InMemoryResponse` is a basic type of response. There are several response types that are wrappers to the `InMemoryResponse`.
>
> For example, `NotFoundReponse` sets the appropriate headers and response code for an `InMemoryResponse` to send an error 404 response to the client.
>
> You can look at the `net.liftweb.http.LiftResponse` to see every type of response provided by Lift.

The third parameter is a list of HTTP cookies, which we will pass a `Nil` value—an empty list—because we don't care about cookies in this case. We passed `200` as the last parameter to define the HTTP response status code.

Now that we know how to build an HTTP response to serve an RSS feed, let's learn how to build the feed content.

To build the feed content, we created the method `getClients`, which builds an XML object using some helper methods. These helper methods format the date and mapping of our list of clients to build XML `item` blocks; each client is an `item` block. So, after iterating the list of clients, it returns the XML that will be used as the parameter when calling the `toRss` method.

See also

▸ You can learn more about how to work with XML using Scala by visiting:

http://www.scala-lang.org/node/131

5
Working with Databases

In this chapter, we will cover the following topics:

- ▶ Configuring a connection to database
- ▶ Mapping a table to a Scala class
- ▶ Creating one-to-many relationships
- ▶ Creating many-to-many relationships
- ▶ Creating CRUD features with CRUDify
- ▶ Paginating result sets
- ▶ Using an in-memory database in application tests

Introduction

We have learned how to create snippets, how to work with forms, and Ajax, how to test your code, and how to create a REST API, and all this is awesome! However, we did not learn how to persist data to make it durable.

In this chapter, we will see how to use Mapper, an **object-relational mapping** (**ORM**) system for relational databases, included with Lift.

The idea is to create a map of database tables into a well-organized structure of objects; for example, if you have a table that holds users, you will have a class that represents the user table.

Let's say that a user can have several phone numbers. Probably, you will have a table containing a column for the phone numbers and a column containing the ID of the user owning that particular phone number.

This means that you will have a class to represent the table that holds phone numbers, and the user class will have an attribute to hold the list of its phone numbers; this is known as a **one-to-many relationship**.

Mapper is a system that helps us build such mappings by providing useful features and abstractions that make working with databases a simple task. For example, Mapper provides several types of fields such as `MappedString`, `MappedInt`, and `MappedDate` which we can use to map the attributes of the class versus the columns in the table being mapped. It also provides useful methods such as `findAll` that is used to get a list of records or save, to persist the data. There is a lot more that Mapper can do, and we'll see what this is through the course of this chapter.

Configuring a connection to database

The first thing we need to learn while working with databases is how to connect the application that we will build with the database itself.

In this recipe, we will show you how to configure Lift to connect with the database of our choice. For this recipe, we will use PostgreSQL; however, other databases can also be used:

Getting ready

1. Start a new blank project.
2. Edit the `build.sbt` file to add the lift-mapper and PostgreSQL driver dependencies:

   ```
   "net.liftweb" %% "lift-mapper" % liftVersion % "compile",
   "org.postgresql" % "postgresql" % "9.2-1003-jdbc4" % "compile"
   ```

3. Create a new database.
4. Create a new user.

How to do it...

Now carry out the following steps to configure a connection with the database:

1. Add the following lines into the `default.props` file:

   ```
   db.driver=org.postgresql.Driver
   db.url=jdbc:postgresql:liftbook
   db.user=<place here the user you've created>
   db.password=<place here the user password>
   ```

2. Add the following `import` statement in the `Boot.scala` file:

   ```
   import net.liftweb.mapper._
   ```

3. Create a new method named `configureDB()` in the `Boot.scala` file with the following code:

```
def configureDB() {
  for {
    driver <- Props.get("db.driver")
    url <- Props.get("db.url")
  } yield {
    val standardVendor =
      new StandardDBVendor(driver, url, Props.get("db.user"),
Props.get("db.password"))

    LiftRules.unloadHooks.append(standardVendor.
closeAllConnections_! _)

    DB.defineConnectionManager(DefaultConnectionIdentifier,
standardVendor)
  }
}
```

4. Then, invoke `configureDB()` from inside the `boot` method.

How it works...

Lift offers the `net.liftweb.mapper.StandardDBVendor` class, which we can use to create connections to the database easily.

This class takes four arguments: driver, URL, user, and password. These are described as follows:

▶ **driver**: The driver argument is the JDBC driver that we will use, that is, `org.postgresql.Driver`

▶ **URL:** The URL argument is the JDBC URL that the driver will use, that is, `jdbc:postgresql:liftbook`

▶ **user** and **password**: The user and password arguments are the values you set when you created the user in the database.

After creating the default vendor, we need to bind it to a **Java Naming and Directory Interface (JNDI)** name that will be used by Lift to manage the connection with the database. To create this bind, we invoked the `defineConnectionManager` method from the `DB` object. This method adds the connection identifier and the database vendor into a HashMap, using the connection identifier as the key and the database vendor as the value. The `DefaultConnectionIdentifier` object provides a default JNDI name that we can use without having to worry about creating our own connection identifier. You can create your own connection identifier if you want. You just need to create an object that extends `ConnectionIdentifier` with a method called `jndiName` that should return a string.

Finally, we told Lift to close all the connections while shutting down the application by appending a function to the `unloadHooks` variable. We did this to avoid locking connections while shutting the application down.

There's more...

It is possible to configure Lift to use a JNDI datasource instead of using the JDBC driver directly. In this way, we can allow the container to create a pool of connections and then tell Lift to use this pool.

To use a JNDI datasource, we will need to perform the following steps:

1. Create a file called `jetty-env.xml` in the `WEB-INF` folder under `src/main/webapp/` with the following content:

```
<!DOCTYPE Configure PUBLIC "-//Jetty//Configure//EN"
"http://www.eclipse.org/jetty/configure.dtd">
<Configure class="org.eclipse.jetty.webapp.WebAppContext">
    <New id="dsliftbook"
class="org.eclipse.jetty.plus.jndi.Resource">
        <Arg>jdbc/dsliftbook</Arg>
        <Arg>
            <New class="org.postgresql.ds.PGSimpleDataSource">
                <Set name="User">place here the user you've
created</Set>
                <Set name="Password">place here the user
password</Set>
                <Set name="DatabaseName">liftbook</Set>
                <Set name="ServerName">localhost</Set>
                <Set name="PortNumber">5432</Set>
            </New>
        </Arg>
    </New>
</Configure>
```

2. Add the following line into the `build.sbt` file:

```
env in Compile := Some(file("./src/main/webapp/WEB-INF/jetty-
env.xml") asFile)
```

3. Remove all the jetty dependencies and add the following:

```
    "org.eclipse.jetty" % "jetty-webapp" %
"8.0.4.v20111024"  % "container",
    "org.eclipse.jetty" % "jetty-plus" % "8.0.4.v20111024"
% "container",
```

4. Add the following code into the `web.xml` file.

```
<resource-ref>
    <res-ref-name>jdbc/dsliftbook</res-ref-name>
    <res-type>javax.sql.DataSource</res-type>
    <res-auth>Container</res-auth>
</resource-ref>
```

5. Remove the `configureDB` method.

6. Replace the invocation of `configureDB` method with the following line of code:

```
DefaultConnectionIdentifier.jndiName = "jdbc/dsliftbook"
```

The creation of the file `jetty-envy.xml` and the change we made in the `web.xml` file were to create the datasource in jetty and make it available to Lift.

Since the connections will be managed by jetty now, we don't need to append hooks so that Lift can close the connections or any other configuration when shutting down the application. All we need to do is tell Lift to get the connections from the JNDI datasource that we have configured into the jetty. We do this by setting the `jndiName` variable of the default connection identifier, `DefaultConnectionIdentifier` as follows:

```
DefaultConnectionIdentifier.jndiName = "jdbc/dsliftbook"
```

The change we've made to the `build.sbt` file was to make the `jetty-env.xml` file available to the embedded jetty. So, we can use it when we get the application started by using the `container:start` command.

See also...

▸ You can learn more about how to configure a JNDI datasource in Jetty at the following address:

```
http://wiki.eclipse.org/Jetty/Howto/Configure_JNDI_Datasource
```

Mapping a table to a Scala class

Now that we know how to connect Lift applications to the database, the next step is to learn how to create mappings between a database table and a Scala object using Mapper.

Getting ready

We will re-use the project we created in the previous recipe since it already has the connection configured.

How to do it...

Carry out the following steps to map a table into a Scala object using Mapper:

1. Create a new file named `Contact.scala` inside the `model` package under `src/main/scala/code/` with the following code:

```scala
package code.model

import net.liftweb.mapper.{MappedString, LongKeyedMetaMapper,
LongKeyedMapper, IdPK}

class Contact extends LongKeyedMapper[Contact] with IdPK {
  def getSingleton = Contact

  object name extends MappedString(this, 100)
}

object Contact extends Contact with LongKeyedMetaMapper[Contact] {
  override def dbTableName = "contacts"
}
```

2. Add the following import statement in the `Boot.scala` file:

```scala
import code.model.Contact
```

3. Add the following code into the `boot` method of the `Boot` class:

```scala
    Schemifier.schemify(
      true, Schemifier.infoF _,
      Contact
    )
```

4. Create a new snippet named `Contacts` with the following code:

```scala
package code.snippet

import code.model.Contact
import scala.xml.Text
import net.liftweb.util.BindHelpers._

class Contacts {
  def prepareContacts_!() {
    Contact.findAll().map(_.delete_!)
    val contactsNames = "John" :: "Joe" :: "Lisa" :: Nil
    contactsNames.foreach(Contact.create.name(_).save())

  }
```

```
def list = {
  prepareContacts_!()

  "li *" #> Contact.findAll().map {
    c => {          c.name.get
    }
  }
}
```

5. Edit the `index.html` file by replacing the content of the `div` element with `main` as the value of `id` using the following code :

```
<div data-list="Contacts.list">
    <ul>
        <li></li>
    </ul>
</div>
```

6. Start the application.

7. Access your local host (`http://localhost:8080`), and you will see a page with three names, as shown in the following screenshot:

How it works...

To work with Mapper, we use a class and an object. The first is the class that is a representation of the table; in this class we define the attributes the object will have based on the columns of the table we are mapping. The second one is the class' companion object where we define some metadata and helper methods.

The `Contact` class extends the `LongKeyedMapper[Contact]` trait and mixes the trait `IdPK`. This means that we are defining a class that has an attribute called `id` (the primary key), and this attribute has the type `Long`. We are also saying that the type of this Mapper is `Contact`.

To define the attributes that our class will have, we need to create objects that extend "something". This "something" is the type of the column. So, when we say an object name extends `MappedString(this, 100)`, we are telling Lift that our `Contact` class will have an attribute called `name`, which will be a string that can be 100 characters long. After defining the basics, we need to tell our Mapper where it can get the metadata about the database table. This is done by defining the `getSingleton` method. The `Contact` object is the object that Mapper uses to get the database table metadata. By default, Lift will use the name of this object as the table name. Since we don't want our table to be called `contact` but `contacts`, we've overridden the method `dbTableName`.

What we have done here is created an object called `Contact`, which is a representation of a table in the database called `contacts` that has two columns: `id` and `name`. Here, `id` is the primary key and of the type `Long`, and `name` is of the type `String`, which will be mapped to a `varchar` datatype.

This is all we need to map a database table to a Scala class, and now that we've got the mapping done, we can use it. To demonstrate how to use the mapping, we have created the snippet `Contacts`.

This snippet has two methods. The `list` method does two things; it first invokes the `prepareContacts_!()` method, and then invokes the `findAll` method from the `Contact` companion object. The `prepareContacts_!()` method also does two things: it first deletes all the contacts from the database and then creates three contacts: `John`, `Joe`, and `Lisa`. To delete all the contacts from the database, it first fetches all of them using the `findAll` method, which executes a `select * from contacts` query and returns a list of `Contact` objects, one for each existing row in the table. Then, it iterates over the collection using the `foreach` method and for each contact, it invokes the delete_! method which as you can imagine will execute a `delete from contacts where id = contactId` query is valid.

After deleting all the contacts from the database table, it iterates the `contactsNames` list, and for each element it invokes the `create` method of the `Contact` companion object, which then creates an instance of the Contact class. Once we have the instance of the `Contact` class, we can set the value of the `name` attribute by passing the value `instance.name(value)`.

You can chain commands while working with Mapper objects because they return themselves. For example, let's say our `Contact` class has `firstName` and `lastName` as attributes. Then, we could do something like this to create and save a new contact:

```
Contact.create.firstName("John").
lastName("Doe").save()
```

Finally, we invoke the `save()` method of the instance, which will make Lift execute an insert query, thus saving the data into the database by creating a new record.

Getting back to the `list` method, we fetch all the contacts again by invoking the `findAll` method, and then create a `li` tag for each contact we have fetched from the database. The content of the `li` tags is the contact name, which we get by calling the `get` method of the attribute we want the value of. So, when you say `contact.name.get`, you are telling Lift that you want to get the value of the `name` attribute from the contact object, which is an instance of the `Contact` class.

There's more...

Lift comes with a variety of built-in field types that we can use; `MappedString` is just one of them. The others include, `MappedInt`, `MappedLong`, and `MappedBoolean`.

All these fields come with some built-in features such as the `toForm` method, which returns the HTML needed to generate a form field, and the `validate` method that validates the value of the field.

By default, Lift will use the name of the object as the name of the table's column; for example, if you define your object as `name`—as we did—Lift will assume that the column name is `name`.

 Lift comes with a built-in list of database-reserved words such as limit, order, user, and so on. If the attribute you are mapping is a database-reserved word, Lift will append _c at the end of the column's name when using `Schemifier`. For example, if you create an attribute called `user`, Lift will create a database column called `user_c`.

You can change this behavior by overriding the `dbColumnName` method, as shown in the following code:

```
object name extends MappedString(this, 100) {
    override def dbColumnName = "some_new_name"
}
```

In this case, we are telling Lift that the name of the column is `some_new_name`. We have seen that you can fetch data from the database using the `findAll` method. However, this method will fetch every single row from the database.

To avoid this, you can filter the result using the `By` object; for example, let's say you want to get only the contacts with the name Joe. To accomplish this, you would add a `By` object as the parameter of the `findAll` method as follows:

```
Contact.findAll(By(Contact.name, "Joe")).
```

There are also other filters such as `ByList` and `NotBy`. And if for some reason the features offered by Mapper to build select queries aren't enough, you can use methods such as `findAllByPreparedStatement` and `findAllByInsecureSQL` where you can use raw SQL to build the queries.

The last thing left to talk about here is how this example would work if we didn't create any table in the database. Well, I hope you remember that we added the following lines of code to the `Boot.scala` file:

```
Schemifier.schemify(
    true, Schemifier.infoF _,
    Contact
)
```

As it turns out, the `Schemifier` object is a helper object that assures that the database has the correct schema based on a list of `MetaMappers`. This means that for each `MetaMapper` we pass to the `Schemifier` object, the object will compare the `MetaMapper` with the database schema and act accordingly so that both the `MetaMapper` and the database schema match. So, in our example, `Schemifier` created the table for us. If you change `MetaMapper` by adding attributes, `Schemifier` will create the proper columns in the table.

See also...

> ▶ To learn more about query parameters, you can find more at:
>
> https://www.assembla.com/spaces/liftweb/wiki/Mapper#querying_the_database

Creating one-to-many relationships

In the previous recipe, we learned how to map a Scala class to a database table using Mapper. However, we have mapped a simple class with only one attribute, and of course, we will not face this while dealing with real-world applications.

We will probably need to work with more complex data such as the one having one-to-many or many-to-many relationships. An example of this kind of relationship would be an application for a store where you'll have customers and orders, and we need to associate each customer with the orders he or she placed. This means that one customer can have many orders.

In this recipe, we will learn how to create such relationships using Mapper.

Getting ready

We will modify the code from the last section by adding a one-to-many relationship into the Contact class. You can use the same project from before or duplicate it and create a new project.

How to do it...

Carry out the following steps:

1. Create a new class named Phone into the model package under src/main/scala/code/ using the following code:

```scala
package code.model

import net.liftweb.mapper._

class Phone extends LongKeyedMapper[Phone] with IdPK {
  def getSingleton = Phone

  object number extends MappedString(this, 20)

  object contact extends MappedLongForeignKey(this, Contact)
}

object Phone extends Phone with LongKeyedMetaMapper[Phone] {
  override def dbTableName = "phones"
}
```

2. Change the Contact class declaration from:

```scala
class Contact extends LongKeyedMapper[Contact] with IdPK
```

To:

```scala
class Contact extends LongKeyedMapper[Contact]
with IdPK
with OneToMany[Long, Contact]
```

3. Add the attribute that will hold the phone numbers to the Contact class as follows:

```scala
object phones extends MappedOneToMany(Phone,
Phone.contact, OrderBy(Phone.id, Ascending)) with
Owned[Phone] with Cascade[Phone]
```

4. Insert the new class into the `Schemifier` list of parameters. It should look like the following code:

```
Schemifier.schemify(
    true, Schemifier.infoF _,
    Contact,
    Phone
)
```

5. In the `Contacts` snippet, replace the `import` statement from the following code:

```
import code.model.Contact
```

To:

```
import code.model._
```

6. Modify the `Contacts.prepareContacts_!` method to associate a phone number to each contact. Your method should be similar to the one in the following lines of code:

```
def prepareContacts_!() {
    Contact.findAll().map(_.delete_!)
    val contactsNames = "John" :: "Joe" :: "Lisa" :: Nil
    val phones = "5555-5555" :: "5555-4444" :: "5555-3333"
:: "5555-2222" :: "5555-1111" :: Nil

    contactsNames.map(name => {
        val contact = Contact.create.name(name)
        val phone = Phone.create.number(phones((new
Random()).nextInt(5))).saveMe()
        contact.phones.append(phone)
        contact.save()
    })
}
```

7. Replace the `list` method's code with the following code:

```
def list = {
    prepareContacts_!()

    ".contact *" #> Contact.findAll().map {
        contact => {
            ".name *" #> contact.name.get &
            ".phone *" #> contact.phones.map(_.number.get)
        }
    }
}
```

8. In the `index.html` file, replace the `ul` tag with the one in the following code snippet:

```
<ul>
        <li class="contact">
            <span class="name"></span>
            <ul>
                <li class="phone"></li>
            </ul>
        </li>
</ul>
```

9. Start the application.

10. Access `http://localhost:8080`.

Now you will see a web page with three names and their phone numbers, as shown in the following screenshot:

How it works...

In order to create a one-to-many relationship, we have mapped a second table called `phone` in the same way we've created the `Contact` class. The difference here is that we have added a new attribute called `contact`. This attribute extends `MappedLongForeignKey`, which is the class that we need to use to tell Lift that this attribute is a foreign key from another table.

In this case, we are telling Lift that `contact` is a foreign key from the `contacts` table in the `phones` table. The first parameter is the owner, which is the class that owns the foreign key, and the second parameter is `MetaMapper`, which maps the parent table.

After mapping the `phones` table and telling Lift that it has a foreign key, we need to tell Lift what the "one" side of the one-to-many relationship will be.

To do this, we need to mix the `OneToMany` trait in the `Contact` class. This trait will add features to manage the one-to-many relationship in the `Contact` class. Then, we need to add one attribute to hold the collection of children records; in other words, we need to add an attribute to hold the contact's phone numbers.

Note that the `phones` attribute extends `MappedOneToMany`, and that the first two parameters of the `MappedOneToMany` constructor are `Phone` and `Phone.contact`. This means that we are telling Lift that this attribute will hold records from the `phones` table and that it should use the `contact` attribute from the `Phone MetaMapper` to do the join. The last parameter, which is optional, is the `OrderBy` object. We've added it to tell Lift that it should order, in an ascending order, the list of phone numbers by their `id`.

We also added a few more traits into the `phones` attribute to show some nice features. One of the traits is `Owned`; this trait tells Lift to delete all orphan fields before saving the record. This means that if, for some reason, there are any records in the child table that has no owner in the parent table, Lift will delete them when you invoke the `save` method, helping you keep your databases consistent and clean.

Another trait we've added is the `Cascade` trait. As its name implies, it tells Lift to delete all the child records while deleting the parent record; for example, if you invoke `contact.delete_!` for a given contact instance, Lift will delete all phone records associated with this contact instance. As you can see, Lift offers an easy and handy way to deal with one-to-many relationships.

See also...

▸ You can read more about one-to-many relationships at the following URL:

`https://www.assembla.com/wiki/show/liftweb/Mapper#onetomany`

Creating many-to-many relationships

Many-to-many relationships are also very common in real-world applications. In this recipe, we will learn how to use Mapper to create such relationships. To do this, we will create a model for a school where we can have one student attending many subjects and one subject having many students.

Getting ready

You can use any of the projects we have used in the previous sections of this chapter. It is up to you whether to change an existing project or duplicate it.

How to do it...

To create a many-to-many relationship, carry out the following steps:

1. Create a class called `Student` in the `model` package with the following code:

```
package code.model

import net.liftweb.mapper._

class Student extends LongKeyedMapper[Student]
with ManyToMany
with IdPK {
  def getSingleton = Student

  object name extends MappedString(this, 50)

  object courses extends MappedManyToMany(CourseStudents,
CourseStudents.student, CourseStudents.course, Course)
}

object Student extends Student with LongKeyedMetaMapper[Student] {
  override def dbTableName = "students"
}
```

2. Create a class called `Course` in the `model` package with the following code:

```
package code.model

import net.liftweb.mapper._

class Course extends LongKeyedMapper[Course]
with ManyToMany
with IdPK {
  def getSingleton = Course

  object name extends MappedString(this, 50)

  object students extends MappedManyToMany(CourseStudents,
CourseStudents.course, CourseStudents.student, Student)
}

object Course extends Course with LongKeyedMetaMapper[Course] {
  override def dbTableName = "courses"

}
```

3. Create a class called `CourseStudents` in the `model` package with the following code:

```
package code.model

import net.liftweb.mapper.{MappedLongForeignKey,
LongKeyedMetaMapper, IdPK, LongKeyedMapper}

class CourseStudents extends LongKeyedMapper[CourseStudents]
with IdPK {
  def getSingleton = CourseStudents

  object course extends MappedLongForeignKey(this, Course)

  object student extends MappedLongForeignKey(this, Student)

}

object CourseStudents extends CourseStudents with LongKeyedMetaMap
per[CourseStudents] {
  override def dbTableName = "courses_students"
}
```

4. Create a new snippet called `Courses`. Here is the code:

```
package code.snippet

import net.liftweb.util.4BindHelpers._
import code.model.{Course, Student}

class Courses {
  def prepareCourses_!() {
    Student.findAll().map(_.delete_!)
    Course.findAll().map(c => {
      c.students.delete_!
      c.delete_!
    })

    val studentNames = "John" :: "Joe" :: "Lisa" :: Nil
    val courseNames = "Math" :: "Biology" :: "Physics" :: Nil

    val students = studentNames.map(student => Student.create.
name(student).saveMe())
```

```
      courseNames.map(courseName => {
        val course = Course.create.name(courseName)
        course.students.appendAll(students)
        course.save
      })
    }

  def list = {
    prepareCourses_!()

    ".course *" #> Course.findAll().map {
      c => {
        ".name *" #> c.name.get &
          ".student *" #> c.students.map(_.name.get)
      }
    }
  }
}
```

5. Add those three classes we created in the `model` package to the `Schemifier` list of parameters as follows:

```
Schemifier.schemify(
  true, Schemifier.infoF _,
  Course,
  Student,
  CourseStudents
)
```

6. Modify the content of `div` with `main` as the value of `id` in the `index.html` file so that it will have the following code:

```
<div data-lift="Courses.list">
    <ul>
        <li class="course">
            <span class="name"></span>
            <ul>
                <li class="student"></li>
            </ul>
        </li>
    </ul>
</div>
```

7. Start the application.

8. Access `http:localhost:8080`.

Now you will see a web page containing a list of courses and its students:

How it works...

To create a many-to-many relationship, we need to set one attribute in each class of the relationship that will be a link to the other class; for example, the `Student` class will have an attribute called `courses`, while the `Course` class will have an attribute called `students`.

However, this is not enough. We will also need a third class, `CourseStudents`, to map the extra table needed to create the many-to-many relationship. This class will have a foreign key for both `Student` and `Courses` classes.

With this is mind, let's take a look at the code we've created and see how it accomplishes the task. The `Course` and `Student` classes are identical since they both mix in the `ManyToMany` trait. This is a trait similar to the `OneToMany` trait in the sense that while the `OneToMany` trait added features to manage one-to-many relationships in the `Contact` class, the `ManyToMany` trait will also add features to manage many-to-many relationships into the `Course` class.

Both classes also define an attribute that extends `MappedManyToMany`, which is a class to track the relationship. The difference between the `Course` and `Student` classes lies in the order of the parameters passed to the `MappedManyToMany` class. The order of the parameters is as follows:

- The class that defines the `CourseStudents` join table is the same for both classes.
- The attribute of the join `Mapper`, `CourseStudents`, which defines the link with the class that is defining the `MappedManyToMany` attribute. In case of the `Course` class, it will be `CourseStudents.course`, while for the `Student` class, it will be `CourseStudents.student`.

- The attribute of the join `Mapper`, `CourseStudents`, which defines the other side of the relation. For the `Course` class, it will be the foreign key of the `Student` class, `CourseStudents.student`, and for the `Student` class, it will be the foreign key of the `Course` class, `CourseStudents.course`.

- The singleton object of the other `Mapper` side of the relation. It will be `Student` for the `Course` class and `Course` for the `Student` class.

This takes care of the first part of the mapping. Now, we need to map the join table, which leads us to the `CourseStudents` class. As you can see, this is a simple mapping which has two attributes and both of them are mapped as `MappedLongForeignKey`. As I said before, this is the class that we need to use to tell Lift that this attribute is a foreign key from another table.

As you can imagine, the join table is a table that has two foreign keys—one for each side of the relation. The snippet uses the `prepareCourses_!` method to clean up the table and create the necessary data to show how the mapping works. You can see that it works just like the example from the *Creating one-to-many relationships* section.

This is true to the `list` method, which just iterates over the list of courses and fetches the list of students for each course, then creates the necessary `CssSel` to render the HTML that will produce the page you saw on the screenshot in the *How to do it...* section of the *Creating many-to-many relationships* recipe. You can see that for a given course, we can get the collection of students directly using `c.students.map(_.name.get)` due to the mapping we've built.

See also...

- You can read more about many-to-many relationships at:

  `https://www.assembla.com/wiki/show/liftweb/Mapper#manytomany`

Creating CRUD features with CRUDify

Another interesting feature offered by Lift is the `CRUDify` trait. Imagine if there was a way to get your mappings and generate all the pages necessary to perform CRUD operations without you having to manually create them one by one. What I am saying is that, given a mapping, your application will automatically have all the pages needed to perform the CRUD operations. Wouldn't it be nice if we had such a feature? Well, it happens that we do have such a feature, as the `CRUDify` trait does exactly this!

 CRUD is an acronym for the four basic functions performed to databases and persistent storage, and it stands for Create, Read, Update, and Destroy.

Getting ready

To demonstrate how the `CRUDify` trait works, we will use the project we created in the *Mapping a table to a Scala class* recipe.

You can duplicate it or just modify the same project.

How to do it...

Carry out the following steps:

1. Mix-in the `CRUDify` trait in the `Contact` object as follows:

   ```
   object Contact extends Contact
   with LongKeyedMetaMapper[Contact]
   ```

2. With `CRUDify[Long, Contact]`, remove the `prepareContacts_!` method from the `Contacts` snippet.

3. Modify the `entries` variable in the `Boot.boot` method to include the `Contact.menus` variable. It should look like the following code:

   ```
    val entries = List(
         Menu.i("Home") / "index" :: // the simple way to declare a
   menu
         // more complex because this menu allows anything in the
         // /static path to be visible
         Menu(Loc("Static", Link(List("static"), true,
   "/static/index"),
           "Static Content")) ::
         Contact.menus
       ).flatten
   ```

4. Start the application.

5. Access `http://localhost:8080`.

At this point, you should see two new menu items **List contacts** and **Create contacts**.

If you click on the **List contacts** link, you will see a web page similar to the following screenshot:

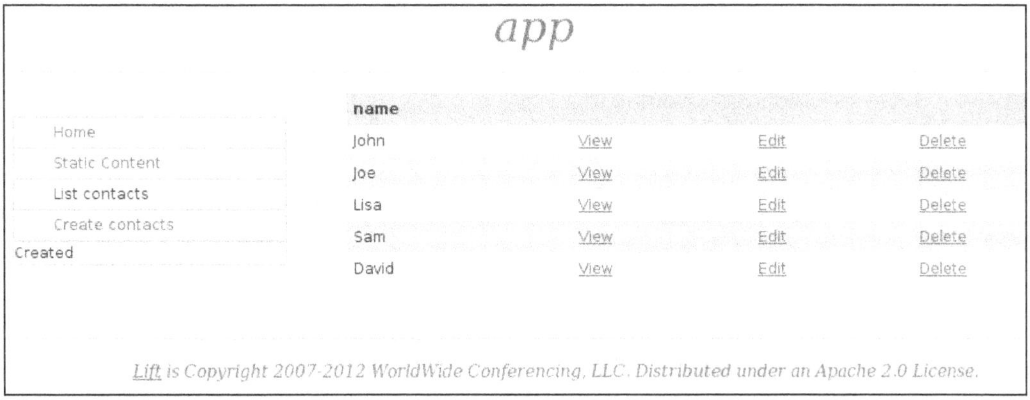

How it works...

Did you see how easy it was to use the CRUDify trait to add the CRUD features in the application? All we needed to do was to add it to the Contact MetaMapper and add the menu entries in the site map.

Let's start with the menu entries. The CRUDify trait comes with a method called menus. This method defines a menu item for each of the CRUD operations—list, edit, create, view, and delete—and binds each of them to a given template, which are defined in the CRUDify trait. For example, when you click on the **List Contacts** link, Lift will use the template defined by the method _showAllTemplate from the CRUDify trait, resulting in the list you saw on the screenshot in the *How to do it...* section in the *Creating CRUD features with CRUDify* recipe. The same holds for each one of the other operations—view, edit, create, and delete. This is why it was so easy to add the CRUD features to the application.

There's more...

You can define your own templates for each of the web pages that are used by the CRUDify trait.

To do this, you need to override the following methods:

- `_viewTemplate`: Override this method to change the template for the **View** page

- `_editTemplate`: Override this method to change the template for the **Edit** page

- `_deleteTemplate`: Override this method to change the template for the **Delete** page

- `_createTemplate`: Override this method to change the template for the **Create contacts** page

- `_showAllTemplate`: Override this method to change the template for the **List contacts** all page

You can also disable the menu entries by defining it's `LocParam` as `Empty`; for example, you can disable the delete menu item by overriding the `deleteMenuLoc` method and making it return `Empty` - `override def deleteMenuLoc = Empty`.

If you do this and try to click on the **Delete** link, you will get an HTTP response with status code **404 Not Found**.

Paginating result sets

Sometimes, we need to deal with so much data that presenting them at once to the user is not an option. The reasons are as follows:

- It will consume too many resources

- It will be slow to render the page to the user

- The user is probably not interested in all the data but just a small part of it

This is why we paginate result sets, to make the user's life easier.

In this section, we will see how to paginate a page using another built-in feature from Lift.

Getting ready

We will use the project from the previous recipe. You can duplicate it or modify the same project.

How to do it...

Carry out the following steps to paginate result sets:

1. In the `Contacts` snippet, add the following `import` statements:

```
import net.liftweb.http.PaginatorSnippet
import net.liftweb.mapper.{MaxRows, StartAt}
```

2. Modify the `Contacts` snippet declaration from:

```
class Contacts {
```

To:

```
object Contacts extends PaginatorSnippet[Contact]
```

3. Add the `count` method.

```
def count = Contact.count
```

4. Override the `itemsPerPage` method:

```
override def itemsPerPage = 3
```

5. Create the `page` method as follows:

```
override def page = Contact.findAll(
  StartAt(curPage * itemsPerPage),
  MaxRows(itemsPerPage)
)
```

6. Modify the `list` method by replacing the invocation to `Contact.findAll()` by the invocation to the `page` method.

```
def list = {
  "li *" #> page.map {
    c => c.name.get
  }
}
}
```

7. Start the application.

8. Access `http://localhost:8080`.

Now you will see a web page similar to the following screenshot:

How it works...

The `PaginatorSnippet` trait provides everything we need to add pagination to a given web page. It calculates how many pages are necessary, the links to the first and last pages, and also the links to the previous and next pages.

The only things we need to do are as follows:

- Define the `count` method, which defines the total number of records the collection that will be paginated has

- Override the `page` method, which is used to retrieve the slice of the collection that will be shown in the current page

We have also overridden the `itemsPerPage` method because we didn't want to use the default value, which is `20`.

The `page` method uses the `curPage` method, which is provided by the `PaginatorSnippet` trait and controls the current page that is being shown to the user. So, by multiplying the value returned from the `curPage` method by the value returned from the `itemsPerPage` method, we can figure out what should be the first record we need to retrieve from the database.

We have also used two query parameters to delimit the range of records that the Mapper should retrieve from the database: the `StartAt` class defines the start point, and the `MaxRows` class defines how many records should be retrieved. This is all it takes in the snippet side to add pagination to a web page. Now, let's take a look at what is necessary to do on the HTML side.

To render the pagination controls in HTML, we need to invoke the `paginate` method from the `PaginatorSnippet` - `<div data-lift="Contacts.paginate">`. This method will bind the `nav` tags and will generate the HTML necessary to create the controls. It will also generate the links with the correct values so that the user can navigate through the web pages.

Each XML tag will generate one control to navigate between the pages :

- The `nav:first` tag will generate the link that takes the user to the first page, it is represented by the **<<** symbol

- The `nav:last` tag will generate the link represented by the **>>** symbol, which takes the user to the last page

- The `nav:prev` and `nav:next` tags will generate the link to go to the previous and next pages respectively. They are represented by the **<** and **>** symbols

- The `nav:allpages` tag will generate all the page numbers with a link so that the user can go directly to the desired page—the current page is represented by a number with no link

- The `nav:records` tag renders the text **Displaying start-end of total**, where **start** is the number of the first record of the current page, **end** is the number of the last record, and **total** is the number of elements in the collection represented by the `count` method

There's more...

You can change the symbols that represent the pagination controls by overriding the following methods, which should return a `NodeSeq object`:

- `prevXml`: It is used for changing the previous page control symbol
- `nextXml`: It is used for changing the next page control symbol
- `firstXml`: It is used for changing the first page control symbol
- `lastXml`: It is used for changing the last page control symbol

Using an in-memory database in application tests

In the previous recipes, we have learned how to use Mapper to map database tables into Scala classes and how to use those classes to communicate with the database.

However, there is a small problem; how to test our application without messing with the database. In other words how can we use a database that provides a controlled environment for tests.

The answer to this is an in-memory database that we can reset every time before running the tests.

Getting ready

We will use the project from the previous section. You can duplicate it or use the same project. You will first need to carry out the following steps:

1. Add the following line in `librariesDependenciesSeq` in the `build.sbt` file:

   ```
   "com.h2database"    % "h2"                    % "1.3.167" %
   "test"
   ```

2. Add the following line at the end of the `build.sbt` file:

   ```
   parallelExecution in Test := false
   ```

3. Create a file named `test.default.props` in props under `src/test/resources/` with the following content:

```
db.driver=org.h2.Driver
db.url=jdbc:h2:mem:liftbook
db.user=sa
db.password=sa
```

4. Create a trait named `InMemoryDB` in `lib` under `src/test/scala/code/` with the following code:

```scala
package code.lib

import code.model.Contact
import net.liftweb.http.LiftRules
import net.liftweb.mapper._
import net.liftweb.util.Props

trait InMemoryDB {
  def prepareDB_!() {
    for {
      driver <- Props.get("db.driver")
      url <- Props.get("db.url")
    } {
      val vendor = new StandardDBVendor(driver, url, Props.
get("db.user"), Props.get("db.password"))
      LiftRules.unloadHooks.append(vendor.closeAllConnections_! _)
      DB.defineConnectionManager(DefaultConnectionIdentifier,
vendor)
    }

    Schemifier.schemify(
      true, Schemifier.infoF _,
      Contact
    )
  }

  def prepareContacts_!() {
    Contact.findAll().map(_.delete_!)
    val contactsNames = "John" :: "Joe" :: "Lisa" :: "Dave" ::
"Sam" :: Nil
    contactsNames.map(Contact.create.name(_).save())

  }

  prepareDB_!()
  prepareContacts_!()
}
```

How to do it...

Now carry out the following steps:

1. Create a class named `ContactsTest` in snippet under `src/test/scala/code/` with the following code:

```
package code.snippet

import org.specs2.mutable.Specification
import code.lib.InMemoryDB

class ContactsTest extends Specification with InMemoryDB {
  "concats snippet" should {
    "retrieve three contacts" in {
      val contacts = Contacts.page
      contacts.size must be equalTo(3)
      contacts.map(_.name).mkString(",") must be
equalTo("John,Joe,Lisa")
    }
  }
}
```

2. Start an `sbt` session.

3. Run the `test` command. After running the test, you should get a result similar to the following screenshot:

```
> test
[info] ContactsTest
[info]
[info] concats snippet should
[info] + retrieve three contacts
[info]
[info]
[info] Total for specification ContactsTest
[info] Finished in 30 ms
[info] 1 example, 0 failure, 0 error
[info]
[info] Passed: : Total 1, Failed 0, Errors 0, Passed 1, Skipped 0
```

How it works...

Since we don't have a JNDI datasource because we are not running the tests with a running jetty instance, we need to configure the database using the JDBC URL.

To configure it, we defined the `test.default.props` file under the `src/test/resources` folder so that the `Props` object could find it and read the values it should use to configure the connection. You can see that the URL we used is `jdbc:h2:mem:liftbook`. This means that we'll connect to an H2 database whose name is `liftbook`. The `mem` parameter is there to tell the H2 database that it should create an in-memory database instead of creating a database in the filesystem.

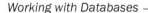

The `InMemoryDB` trait was created to provide the tests with a convenient way to get the database connection for the tests. All you'll need to do is to mix this trait in your test classes and they will have a connection available.

As you can see, this is exactly what we did in the `ContactsTest` specification, and since the connection to the database is available and the `InMemoryDB` trait has created some contacts for us, we can test whether the `Contacts` snippet is doing what it is supposed to do. Since we've invoked the `page` method directly, the `PaginatorSnippet` trait will assume that we are in the first page; so, the `page` method will only return the first three contacts.

There's more...

The modification we did in the `build.sbt` file to prevent parallel execution of tests, that is, `parallelExecution in Test := false`, was to avoid issues during the preparation of the database between the execution of tests.

Imagine if we have two or more tests and they are executed in parallel; this means that while we are executing one test and an instance of the database is created, another test can try to create the same schema in the database where one already exists. This will cause `Schemifier` to throw an exception and the test will fail. This is why we don't want our tests to run in parallel.

6

Working with Record

In this chapter, we will cover the following topics:

- ▸ Configuring a connection to a database using Squeryl
- ▸ Mapping a table to a Scala class
- ▸ Migrating a database using Liquibase
- ▸ Creating one-to-many relationships
- ▸ Creating many-to-many relationships
- ▸ Paginating result sets using Record
- ▸ Testing your application using an in-memory database

Introduction

In the previous chapter, we learned how to store data in a database and how to work with this stored data. However, Mapper is not the only persistent layer available in Lift. In fact, there is another one, named **Record**.

In this chapter, we will learn how to use Record to integrate Lift with **Squeryl**, which is an ORM and **DSL** (**Domain-specific language**), for Scala. Unlike other ORM frameworks that provide a string-based query language, such as JPA-QL and HQL (to mention a few), Squeryl gives us a powerful DSL that we can use to create type-safe access to the database. This means that if you have used any string based query language, when changes to the database are made, you will probably have to deal with runtime errors because the application compiles just fine. But, if you access the database using a DSL that can be checked at compilation time, this means that any changes made to the database and to your models will make your project stop compiling.

While Mappers is a complete ORM framework, Record is a thin layer that you can use to integrate other ORM frameworks with Lift and keep a consistent API. The idea is that, by using Record, your application can have some guarantees; in other words, a record can be created, saved, and presented in different forms (such as XHTML and JSON).

Configuring a connection to a database using Squeryl

The first thing that we need to learn is how to configure Record to create a connection to a database. The database that we will use to build the example and explain how Record works, is PostgreSQL.

Getting ready

Before we can get started, we need to create a new project and carry out basic steps, such as creating a database and a new user.

1. Start a new blank project.
2. Edit the `build.sbt` file to add the `lift-squeryl-record` and `PostgreSQL` driver dependencies, as shown in the following code:

   ```
   "net.liftweb" %% "lift-squeryl-record" % liftVersion % "compile",
   "org.postgresql" % "postgresql" % "9.2-1003-jdbc4"  % "compile"
   ```

3. Create a new database.
4. Create a new user.

How to do it...

1. Add the following lines into the `default.props` file:

   ```
   db.url=jdbc:postgresql:liftbook
   db.user=<place here the user you've created>
   db.password=<place here the user password>
   ```

2. Add the following import statements in the `Boot.scala` file:

   ```
   import net.liftweb.squerylrecord.SquerylRecord
   import org.squeryl.Session
   import java.sql.DriverManager
   import org.squeryl.adapters.PostgreSqlAdapter
   import javax.naming.InitialContext
   import javax.sql.DataSource
   ```

3. Create a new method named `prepareDb` in the `Boot.scala` file, as shown in the following code:

```
def prepareDb() {
  for {
    url <- Props.get("db.url")
    user <- Props.get("db.user")
    pass <- Props.get("db.password")
  }
  SquerylRecord.initWithSquerylSession(Session.create(
    DriverManager.getConnection(url, user, pass),
    new PostgreSqlAdapter))
}
```

4. Then, invoke it from inside the `boot` method:

```
prepareDb()
```

How it works...

The `SquerylRecord` object contains the logic to integrate Record and Squeryl. To initialize the integration, we need to do two things. First, we need to create a `RecordMetaDataFactory` instance, and secondly, we need to create a session.

The session is needed because Squeryl requires every access made to the database to be executed inside the context of the transaction. However, a transaction can only be invoked if a session has already been initialized. On the other hand, `RecordMetaDataFactory` is necessary because it's this factory that makes the integration between Record and Squeryl possible. In other words, this factory makes it possible for Squeryl to use Record objects as its model objects.

The method `initWithSquerylSession` performs the two actions (required to initialize the integration of Record and Squeryl), for us in a convenient way otherwise, we would have had to perform them manually. It calls the `init` method, which creates the `RecordMetaDataFactory` instance and also configures the session. The session that will be configured is the one that is created by invoking the `create` method of the `Session` object. This method takes two arguments. The first argument is the connection object and the second argument is the database adapter, which defines the database dialect. Since we are going to use PostgreSQL as the database, we use the `PostgreSqlAdapter` class, which is responsible for translating the code. Using Squeryl DSL, we write the proper SQL commands into the application.

There's more...

As we did with Mapper, it is also possible to configure Squeryl to use a JNDI Datasource instead of using the JDBC driver directly.

 Be aware that this configuration is for Jetty; it will be different for other containers.

To use a JNDI Datasource, you will need to:

1. Create a file named `jetty-env.xml` in the `WEB-INF` folder with the following content:

```
<!DOCTYPE Configure PUBLIC "-//Jetty//Configure//EN"
  "http://www.eclipse.org/jetty/configure.dtd">
<Configure class="org.eclipse.jetty.webapp.WebAppContext">
    <New id="dsliftbook"
      class="org.eclipse.jetty.plus.jndi.Resource">
      <Arg>jdbc/dsliftbook</Arg>
      <Arg>
        <New class="org.postgresql.ds.PGSimpleDataSource">
          <Set name="User">
            place here the user you've created</Set>
          <Set name="Password">
            place here the user password</Set>
          <Set name="DatabaseName">liftbook</Set>
          <Set name="ServerName">localhost</Set>
          <Set name="PortNumber">5432</Set>
        </New>
      </Arg>
    </New>
</Configure>
```

2. Add the following line into the `build.sbt` file:

```
env in Compile := Some(file("
  ./src/main/webapp/WEB-INF/jetty-env.xml") asFile)
```

3. Remove all Jetty dependencies and add the following code snippet:

```
    "org.eclipse.jetty" % "jetty-webapp" % "8.0.4.v20111024"  %
"container",
    "org.eclipse.jetty" % "jetty-plus" % "8.0.4.v20111024"  %
"container",
```

4. Add the following code into the `web.xml` file:

```
<resource-ref>
    <res-ref-name>jdbc/dsliftbook</res-ref-name>
    <res-type>javax.sql.DataSource</res-type>
    <res-auth>Container</res-auth>
</resource-ref>
```

5. Modify the method `prepareDb` to lookup the JNDI Datasource:

```
val ds = new InitialContext().lookup("java:
    /comp/env/jdbc/dsliftbook").asInstanceOf[DataSource]
```

6. Modify the invocation of the method `initWithSquerylSession`, as follows:

```
SquerylRecord.initWithSquerylSession(
        Session.create(
            ds.getConnection,
            new PostgreSqlAdapter)
    )
```

We have now made all of the changes that we made when configuring Mapper to use the JNDI connection instead of the JDBC one. The only difference is in how we use it. In the case of Mapper, all we needed to do was to set the value for `jndiName` in the `DefaultConnectionIdentifier` object. In the case of Squeryl, we had to lookup the Datasource in `InitialContext`, and after finding the Datasource, we were able to get the connection from it and pass it to the `create` method of the `Session` object.

As you can see, the only difference between using JDBC and JNDI from the code perspective, is how we get the connection to create the Squeryl session. Of course, there is another difference; the connections are now managed by the container.

See also

▸ The *Configuring a connection to a database* recipe in *Chapter 5, Working with Databases*

▸ Learn more about Squeryl at `http://squeryl.org/`

Mapping a table to a Scala class

Now that we have learned how to create a connection to the database using Squeryl and Record, it is time to learn how to map database tables to Scala classes.

Getting ready

Since the project from the previous recipe has the connection already configured, we are going to use it. If for any reason you didn't have the connection to the database configured, please follow the *Configuring a connection to a database using Squeryl* recipe in this chapter.

How to do it...

1. Create a table named `contacts` in the database using the following SQL code snippet:

```
create table contacts (
  id serial not null primary key,
  name varchar(100) not null
)
```

2. Create a new file named `Contact.scala` inside the `model` package, with the following code snippet:

```
package code.model

import net.liftweb.squerylrecord.KeyedRecord
import net.liftweb.squerylrecord.RecordTypeMode._
import net.liftweb.record.{MetaRecord, Record}
import net.liftweb.record.field._
import org.squeryl.annotations.Column

class Contact  extends Record[Contact] with
  KeyedRecord[Long] {
  def meta = Contact

  @Column(name="id")
  override val idField = new LongField(this)

  val name = new StringField(this, "")
}

object Contact extends Contact with MetaRecord[Contact] {
  def selectAll = transaction {
    from(LiftBookSchema.contacts)(c => select (c)).toList
  }

  def delete_!(toDelete: Contact) = transaction {
    LiftBookSchema.contacts.deleteWhere(c => c.id ===
      toDelete.id)
  }

  def create(name: String) = transaction {
    val contact = Contact.createRecord.name(name)

    LiftBookSchema.contacts.insert(contact)
  }
}
```

3. Create a class named `LiftBookSchema` in the `model` package, using the following code snippet:

```
package code.model

import org.squeryl.PrimitiveTypeMode._
import org.squeryl.Schema

object LiftBookSchema extends Schema {
  val contacts = table[Contact]("contacts")

  on(contacts)(s => declare(
    s.id is(autoIncremented("contacts_id_seq"))
  ))
}
```

4. Create a new snippet named `Contacts` with the following code snippet:

```
package code.snippet

import code.model.Contact
import net.liftweb.util.BindHelpers._

class Contacts {
  def prepareContacts_!() {
    Contact.selectAll.map(Contact.delete_! _)
    val contactsNames = "John" :: "Joe" :: "Lisa" :: Nil
    contactsNames.map(Contact.create(_))

  }

  def list = {
    prepareContacts_!()

    "li *" #> Contact.selectAll.map {
      c => c.name.get
    }
  }
}
```

5. Edit the `index.html` file by replacing the content of the `div` with `main` as the value of the `id` field by using the following code snippet:

```
<div data-lift="Contacts.list">
  <ul>
    <li></li>
  </ul>
</div>
```

6. Start the application, access `http://localhost:8080`, and you will see a page with three names, as shown in the following screenshot:

How it works...

I think you have noticed that, unlike when we used `Schemifier` to create the database tables for us, when using Squeryl, we had to create the database tables ourselves. This is because Squeryl does not have a way to incrementally evolve the database structure.

 The Squeryl `schema` object has a method called `create`, which can be used to generate the database structure for the first time. However, it does not do any checks and assumes that there is no table created. So, if you try to run it twice, you'll get an error message saying that the table already exists.

Our `Contact` class extends `Record` and mixes in the `KeyedRecord` trait. When mapping a table to a class using Record, you need to extend `Record`, which is a field container and has helper methods, such as `validate` and `toForm`. As you can imagine, these respectively validate and generate the HTML code that represents the field in a HTML form.

The `KeyedRecord` trait is necessary when the table has a primary key; `KeyedRecord[Long]` means that our primary key is of type `Long`. When you use this trait, you are obligated to override the variable `idField`, which is the primary key itself. We've defined the `idField` variable by assigning the value `LongField(this)` to it. That's because we want a primary key of type `Long`.

 `LongField` is one of the field types provided by Record that defines a field of type `Long`.

Another thing we did to map the primary key was to use the annotation `@Column`, which can be used to define the column metadata. When you say `@Column(name="id")`, you are telling Record that the annotated field represents or is mapped to the table column called `id`. In other words, we are telling Record that the variable `idField` is mapped to the column `id` in the database table.

We have also defined a variable called `name`, which was mapped as a `StringField` object—the type of field is `String`—and since the column's name is the same as the variable name (both are called `name`), we don't need to use the `@Column` annotation. This is because Record, by default, uses the variable name as the column's name.

Finally, we also need to declare the `meta` method, which defines where Record can get the metadata for your class. As you can imagine, defining a `MetaRecord` for your `Record` class requires creating an object and mixing the `MetaRecord` trait into it. That is exactly what we did in this line of code: `object Contact extends Contact with MetaRecord[Contact]`.

There are two differences from Mapper's `meta` objects. First, we don't define the table's metadata (such as the table name) in here, and secondly, since Record is not a complete ORM, Record objects don't have a method to communicate with the database using operations such as `delete`, `insert`, `update`, and `select`. To perform such operations, you need to use methods from Squeryl's `schema` object. This is why we need to create these helper methods to execute `select`, `update`, `delete`, and `insert` operations. Although they are not necessary to use Record with Squeryl, they add a certain level of convenience.

Do you remember that I said that every access made to the database needs to be executed in the context of a transaction? Well, because of this, we need to wrap all methods—`selectAll`, `delete_!(toDelete: Contact)`, and `create(name: String)`—in the `transaction` block. Actually, `transaction` is a method provided by Squeryl which always creates a new transaction. There is another method called `inTransaction` which only creates a new transaction if there are none, and re-uses an existing one otherwise.

When you look at these methods, you will notice that all of them use a variable called `contacts` from the object `LiftBookSchema`. But, what is this schema object and what is this `table` item that we've used to define the variable `contacts`? The `schema` object is the representation of a database schema. In other words, a database schema is a collection of tables, and a Squeryl schema is a collection of all objects that represent database tables.

The definition of tables in Squeryl is by the use of the `table` method. When we created the variable `contacts` by invoking the `table` method, we passed `Contact` (as the type of the table), and the string `contacts`. We said that we wanted to add the table called `contacts`, which should be mapped onto the `Contact` MetaRecord object. So, if you take a look at the `Contact` object, it will be clear what each one of its methods is doing. For example, `LiftBookSchema.contacts.deleteWhere(c => c.id === toDelete.id)`, is going to delete a record from the `contacts` table where the value of `id` for the record matches that for the `Contact` object that is passed as a parameter.

One last thing that we need to do is to map the sequence created by PostgreSQL when we created the table's primary key as being of type `serial`. If we don't do this, we'll get an exception when trying to insert new records into the table. So, we need to tell Squeryl the name of the auto-increment sequence of the `id` field. The `autoIncremented` method takes a string as an argument—the sequence name—and returns an `AutoIncremented` object; a `ColumnAttribute`. Then, we pass this object to the `is` method, which takes `ColumnAttribute` as its argument and returns `ColumnAttributeAssignment`—a class that contains a field and a list of attributes—which contains the field `id` and the auto-increment attribute.

 PostgreSQL usually generates a sequence name of the format `<table-name>_<field-name>_seq`—in our case, `contacts_id_seq`. You might want to confirm this name after creating the table and change it in case of any difference.

There's more...

In order to avoid explicit calling of the `transaction` or `inTransaction` methods all the time, you can tell Lift to do it for you by adding the following code in the `Boot.boot` method:

```
S.addAround(new LoanWrapper {
  override def apply[T](f: => T): T = inTransaction(f)
})
```

You'll also need to add the following import statements in the `Boot.scala` file:

```
import net.liftweb.http.S
import net.liftweb.util.LoanWrapper
import net.liftweb.squerylrecord.RecordTypeMode._
```

And then you can remove the calls to the `inTransaction` method.

See also

▶ Learn more about Squeryl's `insert`, `update`, and `delete` operations at `http://squeryl.org/inserts-updates-delete.html`

▶ For more information on `select`, you can visit `http://squeryl.org/selects.html`

▶ For more information on Squeryl transactions, you can visit `http://squeryl.org/sessions-and-tx.html`

Migrating the database using Liquibase

Squeryl doesn't do database migration for us. This means that you can use the `create` method from the `schema` object only once, because it tries to create all of the tables each time it runs and it will give errors when trying to create a table that already exists.

For this reason, we can use third-party tools such as Liquibase, in order to automate the migration process; that is, database creation and changing. Liquibase uses an XML file, `databaseChangeLog`, to define all of the changes that it needs to execute. Each one of these changes is defined by a `changeSet` tag. It also keeps track of these `changeSet` tags to prevent executing any one of them twice.

Once you define your `databaseChangeLog` file—the XML file that contains the `changeSet` tags—you can tell Lift to execute it during application startup. So, whenever you change your database, all you need to do is to create the `changeSet` tags, add them into the `changelog` file and during the next deployment of your application, your database will be updated. That is what we'll practice doing in this recipe.

Getting ready...

To demonstrate how to use Liquibase to keep your database up to date, let's drop the `contact` table from the database and then recreate it using Liquibase.

1. Add the Liquibase in the `libraryDependencies` section in the `build.sbt` file:

   ```
   "org.liquibase"    %   "liquibase-maven-plugin" % "3.0.2"
   ```

2. In the `Boot` class, add the following method:

   ```
   def runChangeLog(ds: DataSource) {
     val connection = ds.getConnection

     try {
       val database = DatabaseFactory.getInstance().
         findCorrectDatabaseImplementation(new
           JdbcConnection(connection))

       val liquibase = new Liquibase(
         "database/changelog/db.changelog-master.xml",
         new FileSystemResourceAccessor(),
         database
       )
       liquibase.update(null)
     } catch {
       case e: SQLException => {
         connection.rollback()
         throw new DatabaseException(e)
       }
     }
   }
   ```

How to do it...

1. Add the following line into the `prepareDb` method in the `Boot.scala` file, just after the declaration of the `ds` value:

   ```
   runChangeLog(ds)
   ```

2. In the `root` folder—same level as the `src` folder—create a new folder named `database`.

3. Inside the newly created folder, create another new one named `changelog`.

4. Inside the `changelog` folder, create a new file called `db.changelog-master.xml`, containing the following code:

   ```
   <?xml version="1.0" encoding="UTF-8"?>
   <databaseChangeLog
     xmlns="http://www.liquibase.org/xml/ns/dbchangelog/1.9"
     xmlns:xsi="http://www.w3.org/2001/XMLSchema-instance"
     xsi:schemaLocation=
       "http://www.liquibase.org/xml/ns/dbchangelog/1.9
       http://www.liquibase.org/xml/ns/dbchangelog/
         dbchangelog-1.9.xsd">

     <include file="database/changelog/
       db.changelog-1.0.xml"/>
   </databaseChangeLog>
   ```

5. Inside the `changelog` folder, create a new file named `db.changelog-1.0.xml`, containing the following code:

   ```
   <?xml version="1.0" encoding="UTF-8" standalone="no"?>
   <databaseChangeLog xmlns=
     "http://www.liquibase.org/xml/ns/dbchangelog"
     xmlns:xsi="http://www.w3.org/2001/XMLSchema-instance"
     xsi:schemaLocation=
       "http://www.liquibase.org/xml/ns/dbchangelog
       http://www.liquibase.org/xml/ns/dbchangelog/
       dbchangelog-2.0.xsd">
     <changeSet author="author-name" id="1">
       <preConditions onFail="MARK_RAN">
         <not>
           <tableExists tableName="contacts"/>
         </not>
       </preConditions>
   ```

```
        <createTable tableName="contacts">
          <column autoIncrement="true" name="id"
            type="bigserial">
            <constraints nullable="false" primaryKey="true" />
          </column>
          <column name="name" type="varchar(100)"/>
        </createTable>
      </changeSet>
    </databaseChangeLog>
```

6. Start the application.

In the sbt session, you should see a log similar to the log shown in the following screenshot:

```
INFO 5/3/13 7:03 PM:liquibase: Successfully acquired change log lock
INFO 5/3/13 7:03 PM:liquibase: database/changelog/db.changelog-master.xml is using schema version 1.9 rather than version 2.0
INFO 5/3/13 7:03 PM:liquibase: Creating database history table with name: databasechangelog
INFO 5/3/13 7:03 PM:liquibase: Reading from databasechangelog
INFO 5/3/13 7:03 PM:liquibase: Reading from databasechangelog
INFO 5/3/13 7:03 PM:liquibase: ChangeSet database/changelog/db.changelog-1.0.xml::1::author-name ran successfully in 17ms
INFO 5/3/13 7:03 PM:liquibase: Successfully released change log lock
[info] Started SelectChannelConnector@0.0.0.0:8080 STARTING
[success] Total time: 1 s, completed May 3, 2013 7:03:12 PM
```

How it works...

If you check your database after application startup, you'll see three tables—contacts, databasechangelog, and databasechangeloglock.

What happened here, is that when we invoked the runChangelog method during the application startup process, it created an instance of the Liquibase class and then called the update method.

To create the Liquibase instance, you need to pass three arguments to its constructor. The first one is the changelog file—db.changelog-master.xml—which is the file that maps all changeSet tags. The second argument is the ResourceAccessor object, or in other words, how Liquibase will access the changelog file; in our example, we are telling Liquibase that the changelog file should be accessed using the file system and that is why we have used the object FileSystemResourceAccessor. The third parameter is the database object, which is the object that Liquibase will use to communicate with the database.

This method basically does three things. First, it checks for the existence of the tables `databasechangelog` and `databasechangeloglock` and creates them if they do not exist. Secondly, it checks which `changeSet` instances have already been executed so it can execute only new ones, and thirdly, it executes the `changeSet` instances. Each `changeSet` tag describes what needs to be done. In our example, we are telling Liquibase that we want to create a table called `contacts` and that it should have two columns. One is `id` and the other is `name`. After executing the `changeSet`, Liquibase will create a record in the `databasechangelog` table. So, during the next startup, Liquibase will check and discover that the `changeSet` tag was executed and it will not execute it again.

See also

▶ For more details on Liquibase, refer to `http://www.liquibase.org/quickstart.html`

Creating one-to-many relationships

After learning how to map a database table to a Scala class using Record, we will learn how to take the next step, which is mapping a one-to-many relationship using Record.

Getting ready

We are going to modify the project from the last recipe. You can duplicate the project or modify it; it is your choice.

1. Create a table called `phones`:

   ```
   create table phones (
      id serial primary key,
      number varchar(15),
      contact bigint
   )
   ```

2. Add the following import statements in the `Boot.scala` file:

   ```
   import net.liftweb.http.S
   import net.liftweb.util.LoanWrapper
   import net.liftweb.squerylrecord.RecordTypeMode._
   ```

3. Add the following code into the `boot` method in the `Boot.scala` file:

   ```
   S.addAround(new LoanWrapper {
      override def apply[T](f: => T): T = inTransaction(f)
   ```

Now, you won't need to invoke the `inTransaction` or `transaction` methods.

How to do it...

1. In the model folder, create a new file named `Phone.scala` containing the following code:

```scala
package code.model

import net.liftweb.squerylrecord.KeyedRecord
import net.liftweb.record.{MetaRecord, Record}
import net.liftweb.record.field._
import org.squeryl.annotations.Column
import net.liftweb.squerylrecord.RecordTypeMode._
import org.squeryl.dsl.ManyToOne

class Phone private() extends Record[Phone] with
  KeyedRecord[Long] {
  override def meta = Phone

  @Column(name="id")
  override val idField = new LongField(this)

  val number = new StringField(this, "")

  @Column(name="contact")
  val contactId = new LongField(this)

  lazy val contact: ManyToOne[Contact] =
    LiftBookSchema.contactsToPhones.right(this)
}

object Phone extends Phone with MetaRecord[Phone] {
  def selectAll =
    from(LiftBookSchema.phones)(p => select (p)).toList

  def delete_!(toDelete: Phone) =
    LiftBookSchema.phones.deleteWhere
      (p => p.id === toDelete.id)


  def create(number: String) =
    Phone.createRecord.number(number)

}
```

2. Modify the `Contact` class by adding the following code:

```
lazy val phones: OneToMany[Phone] =
  LiftBookSchema.contactsToPhones.left(this)
```

3. Modify the `create` method in the `Contact` object, as follows:

```
def create(name: String, phone: Phone) = {
  val contact = Contact.createRecord.name(name)

  LiftBookSchema.contacts.insert(contact)

  contact.phones.associate(phone)

  contact
}
```

4. Modify the `delete_!` method, as follows:

```
def delete_!(toDelete: Contact) = {
  toDelete.phones.deleteAll
  LiftBookSchema.contacts.deleteWhere
    (c => c.id === toDelete.id)
}
```

5. Modify the `LiftBookSchema` object by adding the following import:

```
import net.liftweb.squerylrecord.RecordTypeMode._
```

6. Also add the following code into the `LiftBookSchema` object:

```
val phones = table[Phone]("phones")

/* phones_id_seq is the name of the sequence generated by
PostgreSQL when using the serial data type */
on(phones)(s => declare(
  s.id is(autoIncremented("phones_id_seq"))
))

val contactsToPhones = oneToManyRelation(contacts,
  phones).via((c, p) => c.id === p.contactId)
```

7. Modify the method `prepareContacts_!()`, in the `Contacts` snippet, as follows:

```
def prepareContacts_!() {
Contact.selectAll.map(Contact.delete_! _)

val contactsNames = "John" :: "Joe" :: "Lisa" :: Nil
val phones = "5555-5555" :: "5555-4444" :: "5555-3333"
  :: "5555-2222" :: "5555-1111" :: Nil
```

```
        contactsNames.map(name => {
          val phone = Phone.create(phones
            ((new Random()).nextInt(5)))
          Contact.create(name, phone)
        })
      }
```

8. In the `Contacts` snippet, modify the method list to look like the following code:

```
def list = {
    prepareContacts_!()

    ".contact *" #> Contact.selectAll.map {
      c => {
        ".name *" #> c.name.get &
        ".phone *" #> c.getPhones.map(_.number.get)
      }
    }
  }
```

9. In the `index.html` file, modify the content of the `div` with `main` as the value of the `id` field using the following code:

```
<div data-lift="Contacts.list">
  <ul>
    <li class="contact">
      <span class="name"></span>
      <ul>
        <li class="phone"></li>
      </ul>
    </li>
  </ul>
</div>
```

10. Start the application and access `http://localhost:8080`; you should see a page similar to the one shown in the following screenshot:

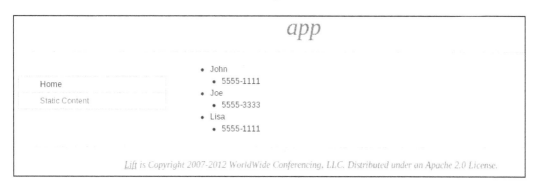

163

How it works...

There is nothing new regarding creation of the `phones` table, the `Phone` class (which is the `Record` class), and the `Phone` object (which is the `MetaRecord` instance). We also had to include the `phones` table in `LiftBookSchema` and define the name of the auto-increment sequence.

However, to create a one-to-many relationship, we need to define a few things.

First of all, we need to create a field called `contactId` in the `Phone` class to hold the foreign key.

Secondly, we need to define the relationship in the schema. We did this by creating the variable `contactsToPhones`, which invokes the `oneToManyRelation` method and builds the relationship between the two tables. The `via` method tells Squeryl which fields on both tables are used to create the relationship and how they are compared—in other words, how the primary key and the foreign key relate to each other.

The last thing that we need to do is define the left side (one-to-many), and the right side (many-to-one). In order to do this, we have created a variable called `contact` in the `Phone` class, and a variable called `phones` in the `Contact` class. The `phones` variable is the left-hand side of the relationship, and that is why we have used the `OneToMany` trait; the `contact` variable is the right-hand side, and we have therefore used the `ManyToOne` trait.

You will notice that both variables use the `OneToManyRelation` object we have declared in the schema.

Now, we can use a helper method provided by traits, such as the `associate` method, which associates the object from the left-hand side with the object from the right-hand side of the relation. This means that by associating a `phone` object with a `contact` object, Squeryl will update the `phone` object, assign the `contactId` field to the `phone` object, and reflect the change in the database.

 One important thing that you must keep in mind is that the `associate` method must be invoked after inserting the parent record in the database, so Squeryl can get the correct ID to insert in the association.

Another method that is available to us is the `deleteAll` method. This method is provided by the `OneToMany` trait. It deletes all of the records from the child table—the right-hand side of the relationship.

Creating many-to-many relationships

So far, we have learned how to map a table using Record and Squeryl; we've also learned how to create a one-to-many relationship. We will now learn how to create a many-to-many relationship using Record and Squeryl.

Getting ready

You can use any of the projects that we have created in this chapter, or you can start a new one; do whatever fits you best.

Create the following tables:

```sql
create table courses (
  id serial primary key,
  name varchar(100)
);

create table students (
  id serial primary key,
  name varchar(100)
);

create table courses_students (
  id serial primary key,
  course bigint,
  student bigint
);
```

How to do it...

1. Create a class called `Student` in the `model` package, as follows:

```scala
package code.model

import net.liftweb.record.{MetaRecord, Record}
import net.liftweb.squerylrecord.KeyedRecord
import net.liftweb.record.field.{StringField, LongField}
import org.squeryl.annotations.Column
import org.squeryl.dsl.ManyToMany
import net.liftweb.squerylrecord.RecordTypeMode._
```

```scala
class Student private() extends Record[Student] with
  KeyedRecord[Long] {
  override def meta = Student

  @Column(name="id")
  override val idField = new LongField(this)

  val name = new StringField(this, "")

  lazy val courses : ManyToMany[Course,CourseStudents] =
    LiftBookSchema.studentCourses.right(this)
}

object Student extends Student with MetaRecord[Student] {
  def selectAll = {
    from(LiftBookSchema.students)(s => select (s)).toList
  }

  def delete(student: Student) = {
    LiftBookSchema.students.deleteWhere(s => s.id
      === student.id)
  }

  def create(name: String) = {
    val student = Student.createRecord.name(name)

    LiftBookSchema.students.insert(student)
  }
}
```

2. Create a class called `Course` using the following code:

```scala
package code.model

import net.liftweb.record.{MetaRecord, Record}
import net.liftweb.squerylrecord.KeyedRecord
import net.liftweb.record.field.{StringField, LongField}
import org.squeryl.annotations.Column
import org.squeryl.dsl.ManyToMany
import net.liftweb.squerylrecord.RecordTypeMode._

class Course private() extends Record[Course] with
  KeyedRecord[Long] {
  override def meta = Course
```

```
  @Column(name="id")
  override val idField = new LongField(this)

  val name = new StringField(this, "")

  lazy val students : ManyToMany[Student,CourseStudents] =
    LiftBookSchema.studentCourses.left(this)

}

object Course extends Course with MetaRecord[Course] {
  def selectAll = {
    from(LiftBookSchema.courses)(c => select (c)).toList
  }

  def delete(course: Course) = {
    LiftBookSchema.courses.deleteWhere(c => c.id
      === course.id)
    LiftBookSchema.studentCourses.deleteWhere(cs =>
      cs.course === course.id)
  }

  def create(name: String) = {
    val course = Course.createRecord.name(name)

    LiftBookSchema.courses.insert(course)
  }

  def createWithStudents(name: String, students:
    List[Student]) = {
    val course = Course.createRecord.name(name)

    LiftBookSchema.courses.insert(course)

    students map { course.students.associate(_) }

    course
  }
}
```

3. Create a class called `CourseStudents`, as shown in the code below:

```
package code.model

import net.liftweb.record.{Record, MetaRecord}
import net.liftweb.squerylrecord.KeyedRecord
import org.squeryl.annotations._
import net.liftweb.record.field.LongField

class CourseStudents extends Record[CourseStudents] with
  KeyedRecord[Long] {
  override def meta = CourseStudents

  @Column(name="id")
  override val idField = new LongField(this)

  val course = new LongField(this)

  val student = new LongField(this)
}

object CourseStudents extends CourseStudents with
MetaRecord[CourseStudents] {

}
```

4. Add the `students` and `courses` classes into the `LiftBookSchema` object, as shown in the code below:

```
object LiftBookSchema extends Schema {
  val students = table[Student]("students")
  val courses = table[Course]("courses")

  val studentCourses = manyToManyRelation(courses,
    students, "courses_students").via[CourseStudents] {

(courseTable, studentTable, courseStudentsTable) =>
  (courseStudentsTable.course === courseTable.id,
  cs.student === studentTable.id)
  } on(students)(s => declare(
    s.id is(autoIncremented("students_id_seq"))
  ))
```

```
  on(courses)(c => declare(
    c.id is(autoIncremented("courses_id_seq"))
  ))

  on(studentCourses)(s => declare(
    s.id is (autoIncremented("courses_students_id_seq"))
  ))
}
```

5. Create a new snippet called `Courses`, as shown in the code below:

```
package code.snippet

import code.model._
import net.liftweb.util.BindHelpers._

class Courses {
  def prepareCourses_!() {
    Student.selectAll map { Student.delete(_) }
    Course.selectAll map { Course.delete(_) }

    val studentNames = "John" :: "Joe" :: "Lisa" :: Nil
    val courseNames = "Math" :: "Biology" ::
      "Physics" :: Nil

    val students = studentNames map {  Student.create(_) }

    courseNames map { Course.createWithStudents
      (_, students) }
  }

  def list = {
    prepareCourses_!()

    ".course *" #> Course.selectAll.map {
      c => {
        ".name *" #> c.name.get &
          ".student *" #> c.students.map(_.name.get)
      }
    }
  }
}
```

6. In the `index.html` file, replace the content of the `div` with `main` as the value of the `id` field, with the following code:

```
<div data-lift="Courses.list">
  <ul>
    <li class="course">
      <span class="name"></span>
      <ul>
        <li class="student"></li>
      </ul>
    </li>
  </ul>
</div>
```

7. Start the application, access `http:localhost:8080`, and you will see a page similar to the one shown in the following screenshot:

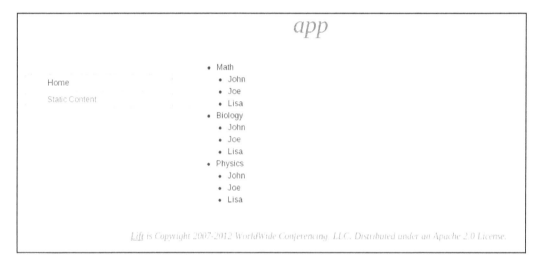

How it works...

Let's start with the class that glues `students` and `courses` together: `CourseStudents`. You can see that it is a regular mapping, just like the one we created in the second recipe of this chapter, *Mapping a table to a Scala class*. So, if this class is just a normal class, how does Record know how to put the pieces together?

Well, if you take a look at the `LiftBookSchema` object, you will see that, besides the code to set the auto-increment keys, we also declared a variable called `studendCourses` by invoking the `manyToManyRelation` method. This method takes three arguments. The first one is the left-hand table, `courses`; the second argument is the right-hand table, `students`, and the third argument is the name of the middle table, or the table that will hold the relationship between the other two. Note, that the argument is the name of the table as it is in the database.

Having one instance of the `ManyToManyBuilder` object, we can invoke the method called `via`, which will define the relationship between the primary and foreign keys of the three tables. To invoke the `via` method, we need to inform Squeryl about the class that maps the middle table; in our case, this is the `CourseStudents` class. Then, we need to pass a block containing a function that takes three arguments and returns a pair of `EqualityExpression` objects. In other words, we need to tell Squeryl how to compare the keys. The first argument, `courseTable`, is the left-hand table, the second one, `studentTable`, is the right-hand table, and the third argument, `courseStudentsTable`, is the middle table. The pair of equality expressions is compounded by `courseStudentsTable.course === course.id` and `courseStudentsTabl.student === student.id`. The first expression tells Squeryl that the relation between the tables, `CourseStudents` and `Course`, is defined by equality between the `id` field of the `Course` table and the `course` field of the `CourseStudents` table. The second expression states that the relationship between the `Student` table and the `CourseStudents` table is given by the equality between the `id` field of the `student` table and the `student` field of the `CourseStudents` table.

The last part of the mapping is to define the fields in both tables, `Student` and `Course`, so that we can query course data of a given student or student data of a given course. For this, we need to define a variable in both classes. In the `Course` class, we need to create a variable to hold the students that are attending, and in the `Student` class, we need to set a variable to hold the courses that the student is enrolled on. In the `Course` class we've added `val students`, which has the type `ManyToMany[Student, CourseStudents]` and is built by invoking the `left` method of the many-to-many relationship defined by the class `CourseStudents`. We are using the `left` method in the `Course` class, because we defined the `Course` class as the left-hand side of the relationship when we defined the relationship in the `LiftBookSchema` class as `manyToManyRelation(courses, students, "courses_students")`. This method returns a `Query[R]` with `ManyToMany`, which means that we can query records from the right-hand table, `Student`, from this variable.

On the other hand, in the `Student` class we need to define a variable of type `ManyToMany[Course, CourseStudents]` to hold the `ManyToMany` object. Since the `Student` class was defined as the right-hand table, we will use the `right` method.

Note, that these variable types are defined in terms of the other table and the middle table. So, in the `Student` class, we defined it as `ManyToMany[Course, CourseStudents]`, and in the `Course` table, we defined it as `ManyToMany[Student, CourseStudents]`.

All of the other methods we created in the `Student` and `Course` classes are helper methods that were created so that we could create, delete, and query the data in an easier way.

We have seen all of these methods in the previous section, which you can refer to, if you need to find a specific detail that you might have forgotten.

Paginating result sets using Record

In *Chapter 5*, *Working with Databases*, we have seen how to paginate result sets using `PaginatorSnippet` and Mapper, in the *Paginating result sets* recipe. We'll be using the `PaginatorSnippet` tool, so there will be nothing new in that sense; however, Record does not have the helper methods that Mapper does. Therefore, paginating the result sets using Record and Squeryl is a little different.

In this recipe we will look at these differences and learn how to paginate result sets using Squeryl.

Getting ready

To keep things simple and to focus on what is important, we will use the project from the second recipe of this chapter, *Mapping a table to a Scala class*, where we mapped the `contacts` table. You can create a new project by duplicating the old one or you can modify it.

How to do it...

Perform the following steps to paginate a result set using Record and Squeryl:

1. Modify the `Contact` class by adding the following method definitions:

   ```
   def count = {
     from(LiftBookSchema.contacts)(c =>
       compute(countDistinct(c.id))).toLong
   }

   def selectAll(offset: Int, itemsPerPage: Int) = {
     from(LiftBookSchema.contacts)(c => select
       (c)).page(offset, itemsPerPage).toList
   }
   ```

2. Import `PaginatorSnippet` into the `Contacts` snippet, as shown in the following code:

   ```
   import net.liftweb.http.PaginatorSnippet
   ```

3. Modify the `Contacts` snippet by adding the following method definitions:

   ```
   def count = Contact.count

   override def itemsPerPage = 3

   def page = Contact.selectAll(
     curPage * itemsPerPage,
     itemsPerPage
   )
   ```

4. Add some more names into the `contactsNames` variable, as shown in the following code:

```
val contactsNames = "John" :: "Joe" :: "Lisa" ::
  "Damien" :: "Adam" :: Nil
```

5. Change the `list` method by replacing the invocation for the `selectAll` method with that for the `page` method:

```
def list = {
prepareContacts_!()

"li *" #> page.map {
  c => c.name.get
}
}
```

6. In the `index.html` file, add the following code after the `div` tag with the attribute `data-lift="Contacts.list"`:

```
<div class="l:Contacts.paginate">
    <nav:first></nav:first>
    |
    <nav:prev></nav:prev>
    |
    <nav:allpages> | </nav:allpages>
    |
    <nav:next></nav:next>
    |
    <nav:last></nav:last>

    <p><nav:records></nav:records></p>
</div>
```

7. Start the application.

8. Access `http://localhost:8080`, to see the results on a page similar to the following screenshot:

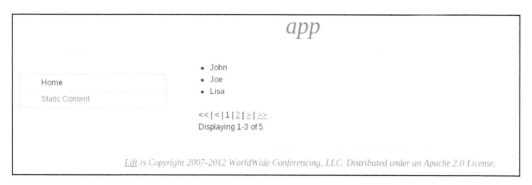

How it works...

As already stated in the introduction of the recipe, we are using the same `PaginatorSnippet` instance that we used in *Chapter 5, Working with Databases*. This means that we need to define the `count` and `page` methods and add the proper tags in the HTML file in order to get Lift to render the pagination controls.

If you compare the code from this recipe with the code from *Chapter 5, Working with Databases*, you will see that they are almost the same and the differences are in the `count` and `page` methods. These differences are due to the fact that Record is not a complete ORM, like Mapper is. This means that the `Record` class does not have the `count` or `selectAll` methods, which respectively take an offset value and a limit value as argument. That is why we needed to create those methods ourselves.

You can see that the `count` method is quite similar to the `selectAll` method; the difference is that instead of invoking the `select` method we invoke two other methods, namely, `compute` and `countDistinct`. Note that in the new version of the `selectAll` method, we added the call to the `page` method between the calls to the `select` and `toList` methods, passing the offset and items per page values as arguments. As you can imagine, Squeryl will limit the result set, taking into account those parameters.

See also

▶   The *Paginating result sets* recipe in *Chapter 5, Working with Databases*

Testing your application using an in-memory database

Until now, we have learned how to integrate our Lift application with the database using Record and Squeryl. Now it is time to learn, similar to what we did in *Chapter 5, Working with Databases*, about how to test an application that uses these two components: Record and Squeryl.

Getting ready

We will modify the project that we have worked on in the previous recipe. Again, you can modify it directly or create a new one by duplicating it.

How to do it...

To modify an old or a new project, perform the following steps:

1. Add `h2` as a new dependency into the `Seq libraryDependencies` section in the `build.sbt` file:

   ```
   "com.h2database"    % "h2"                    %
      "1.3.167" % "test"
   ```

2. In the `build.sbt` file, set `sbt` to not execute tests in parallel using the following command:

   ```
   parallelExecution in Test := false
   ```

3. In the `test | resources` folder, create a new folder called `props` and then inside this folder, create a file called `test.default.props` using the following key/value pairs:

   ```
   db.url=jdbc:h2:mem:liftbook;DB_CLOSE_DELAY=-1
   db.user=sa
   db.password=
   ```

To test your application using an in-memory database, carry out the following steps:

1. In the `\test\scala` folder, create (inside the `code.lib` package), a new trait called `InMemoryDB`, using the following code:

   ```
   package code.lib

   import net.liftweb.util.Props
   import code.model.{LiftBookSchema, Contact}
   import org.squeryl.adapters.H2Adapter
   import java.sql.DriverManager
   import org.squeryl.Session
   import net.liftweb.squerylrecord.SquerylRecord

   import net.liftweb.squerylrecord.RecordTypeMode._

   trait InMemoryDB {
     def prepareDB_!() {
       for {
         url <- Props.get("db.url")
         user <- Props.get("db.user")
         pass <- Props.get("db.password")
       } {
         SquerylRecord.initWithSquerylSession(
           Session.create(
   ```

```
        DriverManager.getConnection(url, user, pass),
        new H2Adapter
        )
      )
    }

    inTransaction {
      LiftBookSchema.drop
      LiftBookSchema.create
    }
  }

  def prepareContacts_!() {
    inTransaction {
      val contactsNames = "John" :: "Joe" :: "Lisa" ::
        "Dave" :: "Sam" :: Nil
      contactsNames.map(Contact.create(_))
    }
  }

  prepareDB_!()
  prepareContacts_!()
}
```

2. In the \test\scala folder, create (inside the code.snippet package), a new class called ContactsTest, using the following code:

```
package code.snippet

import org.specs2.mutable.Specification
import code.lib.InMemoryDB
import net.liftweb.squerylrecord.RecordTypeMode._

class ContactsTest extends Specification with InMemoryDB {
  "concats snippet" should {
    "retrieve three contacts" in {
      inTransaction {
        val contacts = Contacts.page
        contacts.size must be equalTo(3)
        contacts.map(_.name).mkString(",") must be
          equalTo("John,Joe,Lisa")
      }
    }
  }
}
```

3. Run the `test` command in an `sbt` session. After `sbt` finishes running the test, you should see a result similar to that shown in the following screenshot:

```
[info] ContactsTest
[info]
[info] concats snippet should
[info] + retrieve three contacts
[info]
[info]
[info] Total for specification ContactsTest
[info] Finished in 24 ms
[info] 1 example, 0 failure, 0 error
[info]
[info] Passed: : Total 1, Failed 0, Errors 0, Passed 1, Skipped 0
[success] Total time: 4 s, completed May 11, 2013 3:35:18 PM
```

How it works...

You can see that we have created a trait so that we can have a convenient way to set up the in-memory database for tests that require a database. All it needs to do is mix the `InMemoryDB` trait in.

This trait invokes two methods: `prepareDB_!()` and `prepareContacts_!()`.

The `prepareDB_!()` method creates a connection with the database and initializes a Squeryl session. The connection with the database is created in the same way as in the first recipe of this chapter. With the initialized session, the `prepareDB_!()` method drops the existing schema and creates a new one. Therefore, every `class` will have a freshly created database schema.

The reason why we have used the `drop` and `create` methods of the Squeryl schema in these tests is that we want the database to be recreated, and to be sure that our tests, environment is controlled and that one test is not affecting the others.

Then, with the newly created schema, the trait invokes the `prepareContacts_!()` method, which creates all of the data needed to run the test.

See also

▸ The *Testing snippets using Specs2* recipe in *Chapter 2, Working with HTML*

▸ The *Testing a REST service using Specs2* recipe in *Chapter 4, Working with REST*

▸ The *Configuring a connection to a database using Squeryl* recipe in this chapter

▸ The *Using an in-memory database in application tests* recipe in *Chapter 5, Working with Databases*

7
Working with MongoDB

In this chapter, we will cover the following recipes:

- ▸ Connecting to MongoDB using Record
- ▸ Mapping a MongoDB collection to a Scala class
- ▸ Mapping embedded objects
- ▸ Mapping referenced objects
- ▸ Querying with Rogue

Introduction

NoSQL databases are very common nowadays. This is because they focus on having low latency and high throughput. This is very important due to the high volume of data that some applications have to deal with.

One of the popular NoSQL databases is MongoDB, an open source document database that is written in C++ and that stores data in the binary form of JSON objects, **BSON**. MongoDB has some features such as supporting autosharding which mean that it can scale horizontally, and support GridFS, which is a specification for storing data that exceeds the size limit of a BSON document (16 MB).

Connecting to MongoDB using record

In this recipe, we will see how we can use `record` to connect our Lift application to a MongoDB database.

Getting ready

Before starting with this recipe, you will need to install MongoDB on your computer. You can download the appropriate installer for your OS from `http://www.mongodb.org/downloads`, and you can find installation instructions specific to your OS at `http://docs.mongodb.org/manual/installation/`.

How to do it...

1. Start a new blank project.

2. Edit the `build.sbt` file and add the following dependencies:

   ```
   "net.liftweb"
           %% "lift-mongodb"          % liftVersion          %
   "compile->default" withSources(),
   "net.liftweb"
           %% "lift-mongodb-record"  % liftVersion          %
   "compile->default" withSources()
   ```

3. Add the following `import` statements in the `Boot.scala` file:

   ```
   import net.liftweb.mongodb.{DefaultMongoIdentifier, MongoDB}
   import com.mongodb.Mongo
   ```

4. Add the following line in the `Boot.boot` method:

   ```
   MongoDB.defineDb(DefaultMongoIdentifier, new Mongo, "liftbook")
   ```

5. Start the MongoDB server.

6. Start the application.

How it works...

Lift provides an efficient layer to integrate applications with MongoDB. You can see that creating a connection to a MongoDB database is easy, and it takes just one line of code: `MongoDB.defineDb(DefaultMongoIdentifier, new Mongo, "liftbook")`.

The `defineDb` method takes three arguments. The first one is an identifier and defines a JNDI name for the Mongo instance. This argument is used by Lift as a key of a HashMap of identifiers to addresses. Therefore, given an identifier, Lift can reach the correct Mongo instance.

 The fact that Lift keeps this HashMap means that we can set more than one instance.

The second argument is the Mongo instance `new Mongo()`. You can see that we didn't pass any parameter when constructing the `Mongo` object instance. This means that Lift will create a Mongo instance using `localhost` as the host address and the default Mongo port, `27017`. Finally, the third parameter is the database name.

 It is really easy to use MongoDB on a Lift application. One line of code is all you need to connect your application to a MongoDB database.

Mapping a MongoDB collection to a Scala class

In the previous recipe, we learned how to connect a Lift application to a MongoDB database. Now, we will learn how to map a collection from MongoDB to a Scala class so we can use it to store and retrieve data into and from the MongoDB collection.

Getting ready

Let's modify the project from the previous recipe because it already has the connection configured.

How to do it...

Carry out the following steps:

1. Create a file named `Contact.scala` in the `model` package using the following code:

```scala
package code.model

import net.liftweb.mongodb.record._
import net.liftweb.mongodb.record.field._
import net.liftweb.record.field.StringField

class Contact extends MongoRecord[Contact] with
ObjectIdPk[Contact] {
  def meta = Contact

  object name extends StringField(this, 150)
}

object Contact extends Contact with MongoMetaRecord[Contact]
```

2. Create a file named `Contacts.scala` in the `snippet` package with the following code:

```
package code.snippet

import code.model._
import net.liftweb.util.BindHelpers._

class Contacts {
  def prepareContacts_!() {
    Contact.findAll.map(_.delete_!)
    val contactsNames = "John" :: "Joe" :: "Lisa" :: Nil
    contactsNames.map(Contact.createRecord.name(_).save)
  }

  def list = {
    prepareContacts_!()

    "li *" #> Contact.findAll.map {
      c => c.name.get
    }
  }
}
```

3. In the `index.html` file, modify the `div` tag with `id` set to `main` such that it has the following code:

```
<div data-lift="Contacts.list">
        <ul>
            <li></li>
        </ul>
    </div>
```

4. Start the application.

5. Access `http://localhost:8080` via your browser. You should see a list of contacts as shown in in the following screenshot:

How it works...

If you compare the code from the *Connection to MongoDB using record* recipe with the code from this recipe, you can see that when using `MongoRecord`, we did not need to declare all those helper methods we had to declare with `record` and Squeryl. Another difference between working with `record` and Squeryl and working with `record` and MongoDB is how we create the map. In the case of `record` and Squeryl, we had to extend `record` and mix `KeyedRecord` into the class that will represent our table. On the other hand, when working with Mongo, we needed to extend `MongoRecord` and mix `ObjectIdPk` in. For the object that will hold the metadata, we extended `MetaRecord` in the case of `record` with Squeryl, and `MongoMetaRecord` when working with MongoDB and `record`.

See also

- ▶ Learn more about MongoDB at `http://www.mongodb.org/`
- ▶ Learn more about Lift and MongoDB at the following URLs:

   - ❑ `https://www.assembla.com/wiki/show/liftweb/Mongo_Record_Basics`
   - ❑ `https://www.assembla.com/wiki/show/liftweb/Mongo_Record_Referenced_Objects`
   - ❑ `https://www.assembla.com/wiki/show/liftweb/Mongo_Record_Embedded_Objects`
   - ❑ `https://www.assembla.com/wiki/show/liftweb/MongoDB`
   - ❑ `https://www.assembla.com/wiki/show/liftweb/lift-mongodb`

Mapping embedded objects

When working with document-based databases such as MongoDB, instead of using a one-to-many relationship to link to classes that represent two tables in the database—such as `contacts` and `phones`—we can map both objects `Contact` and `Phone`. Then, instead of storing them in two different collections, we embed the `phone` object into the `contact` object. In the following recipe, we will learn how to embed one object into another.

Getting ready

We'll keep evolving the project from the previous recipe.

How to do it...

Carry out the following steps:

1. Create a new file named `Phone.scala` in `src/main/scala/code/model` with the following code:

```scala
package code.model

import net.liftweb.mongodb.record._
import net.liftweb.record.field.StringField

class Phone extends BsonRecord[Phone] {
  def meta = Phone

  val number = new StringField(this, 15)
}

object Phone extends Phone with BsonMetaRecord[Phone]
```

2. Change the `Contact` class by adding the `numbers` object as follows:

```scala
class Contact extends MongoRecord[Contact] with
ObjectIdPk[Contact] {
  def meta = Contact

  object name extends StringField(this, 150)

  object numbers extends BsonRecordListField(this, Phone)
}
```

3. Change the `Contacts` snippet as follows:

```scala
class Contacts {
  private def createContact(name: String, phoneNumbers:
List[String]) {
    val phones = phoneNumbers.map(Phone.createRecord.number(_))
    Contact.createRecord.name(name).numbers(phones).save
  }

  def prepareContacts_!() {
    Contact.findAll.map(_.delete_!)
    createContact("John", "555-5555" :: Nil)
    createContact("Joe", "444-4444" :: "222-2222" :: Nil)
    createContact("Lisa", "333-3333" :: Nil)
  }
```

```
def list = {
  prepareContacts_!()

  "li *" #> Contact.findAll.map {
    contact => {
      ".name *" #> contact.name.get &
        ".phone *" #> contact.numbers.get.map(_.number.get)
    }
  }
}
```

4. Change the `ul` tag in the `index.html` file as follows:

```
<ul>
    <li>
        <span class="name"></span>
        <ul>
            <li class="phone"></li>
        </ul>
    </li>
</ul>
```

5. Start the application.

6. Access `http://localhost:8080` and you'll see a web page such as the one shown in the following screenshot:

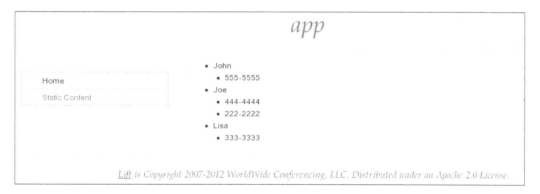

How it works...

The first thing to notice is that while the `Contact` class extends `MongoRecord`, the `Phone` class extends `BsonRecord`, which is a special type of `Record` that is used to encode and decode BSON/DBObject objects. This means that Lift will know how to convert the BSON representation of a phone number—which is the format that MongoDB uses to save the data—into a DBObject, which is a key-value map that can be saved in the database.

One important difference between the `MongoRecord` and `BsonRecord` traits is that the latter can't save itself, while the former can. The consequence of this difference is that we can't invoke the `save` or `saveTheRecord` methods of a `BsonRecord` object. Thus, the only thing we can do is to embed it in a `MongoRecord` object.

Another difference between the `Phone` and `Contact` classes is their companion object. In the `Contact` class, we extended `MongoRecord`, and its companion object extended the `MongoMetaRecord` trait. In the `Phone` class, we extended `BsonRecord`, and its companion object extended the `BsonMetaRecord` trait. As you can imagine, `MongoMetaRecord` is used to deal with `MongoRecord` objects, and `BsonMetaRecord` is used to deal with `BsonRecord` objects.

So, if the only thing we can do with `BsonRecord` is to embed it into `MongoRecord`, how do we do it?

If you take a look at the `Contact` class, you'll see that the `numbers` object we added extends the `BsonRecordListField` class, which can hold a list of `BsonRecord` objects.

Note that the `BsonRecordListField` class takes two arguments, the first one being the owner—that's why we passed the value `this`—and the second argument being the object we want to embed, in this case, the `Phone` object's `BsonMetaRecord` trait.

There's more...

We have embeded a list of `Phone` objects into the `Contact` class. But, what if you just want to embed one object instead of a list? In this case, you can use the `BsonRecordField` class.

The difference between the `BsonRecordListField` and `BsonRecordField` classes is that the latter contains only one object, while the former can contain one or more objects. This means that when saving the data into MongoDB, the `BsonRecordField` class will be saved as a subobject and `BsonRecordListField` will be saved as an array of objects.

See also

- You can learn more about BSON objects at `http://docs.mongodb.org/meta-driver/latest/legacy/bson/`
- You can learn more about embedded objects in Lift at `https://www.assembla.com/spaces/liftweb/wiki/Mongo_Record_Embedded_Objects`

Mapping referenced objects

In the last recipe, we learned how to embed one object into another using `record`. However, there are situations where it's better to just create a reference from one object to another. For example, let's say we are creating a system for a store and we'll need to generate some reports. It's not practical to embed order into the clients because if we did so, each time we wanted to generate a report related to orders only, we would have to fetch all clients to find the order in which we want to generate the report. So, in such situations, it makes more sense to create a reference between clients and their orders. This is what we'll learn in this recipe.

Getting ready

We'll evolve the project we used in the *Connecting to MongoDB using record* recipe. You can duplicate or modify it.

How to do it...

Carry out the following steps:

1. Create a file called `Order.scala` under `src/main/scala/code/model` with the following code:

```
package code.model

import net.liftweb.mongodb.record._
import net.liftweb.mongodb.record.field._
import net.liftweb.record.field._

class Order extends MongoRecord[Order] with ObjectIdPk[Order] {
  def meta = Order

  object date extends DateField(this)

  object total extends DoubleField(this)

}

object Order extends Order with MongoMetaRecord[Order]
```

2. Create a file called `Client.scala` under `src/main/scala/code/model` with the following code:

```
package code.model

import net.liftweb.mongodb.record._
import net.liftweb.mongodb.record.field._
import net.liftweb.record.field.StringField
```

```
class Client extends MongoRecord[Client] with ObjectIdPk[Client] {
  def meta = Client

  object name extends StringField(this, 150)

  object orders extends ObjectIdRefListField(this, Order)
}

object Client extends Client with MongoMetaRecord[Client]
```

3. Create a file called `Clients.scala` under `src/main/scala/code/snippet` with the following code:

```
package code.snippet

import code.model._
import net.liftweb.util.BindHelpers._
import java.util.Date
import java.text.SimpleDateFormat

class Clients {
  val dateFormat = new SimpleDateFormat("dd/MM/yyyy")
  def prepareOrders(client: Client, totalValue: Double) {
    val order = Order.createRecord.date(new Date()).
total(totalValue).saveTheRecord().get

    client.orders(order.id.get :: Nil).save
  }

  def prepareClients() {
    Client.findAll.map(_.delete_!)
    Order.findAll.map(_.delete_!)

    Client.createRecord.name("John").saveTheRecord().
map(prepareOrders(_, 250.23))
    Client.createRecord.name("Joe").saveTheRecord().
map(prepareOrders(_, 100.00))
    Client.createRecord.name("Lisa").saveTheRecord().
map(prepareOrders(_, 75.78))
  }

  def list = {
    prepareClients()

    "li *" #> Client.findAll.map { client =>
```

```
".name *" #> client.name.get &
  ".orders *" #> client.orders.objs.map { order =>
    "Date: " + dateFormat.format(order.date.get) + " -
value: $ " + order.total.get
        }
      }
    }
  }
```

4. Replace the contents of the div tag with id set to main in the index.html file using the following HTML snippet:

```
<div data-lift="Clients.list">
    <ul>
        <li>
            <span class="name"></span>
            <ul>
                <li class="orders"></li>
            </ul>
        </li>
    </ul>
</div>
```

5. Start the application.

6. Access http://localhost:8080 and you'll see a web page like the one in the following screenshot:

How it works...

The difference between this technique and the one mentioned in the *Mapping embedded objects* recipe is that, to reference an object in this technique, the needs to exist in its own collection, while to embed an object inside another, the object to be embedded needs to exist only inside the object that contains it—its owner. Since we need to save the object we'll be referencing in its own collection, it has to be a MongoRecord object. Thus, everything that we learned in the *Mapping embedded objects* recipe holds true here.

So, as you can see, there is nothing new regarding the mapping of the `Client` and `Order` classes, except for the fact that we mapped the `order` attribute of the `Client` class as an object that extends `ObjectIdRefListField`. To use the `ObjectIdRefListField` class, we had to pass two parameters to its constructor. The first parameter is the owner of the reference, in this case, the `Client` object (that is why we passed `this` as the first parameter). The second parameter is the object that we want to reference `Order`.

When we used `object orders extends ObjectIdRefListField(this, Order)`, we told `record` that the `Client` object will hold a reference to a list of `Order` objects. You might think that this is very similar to embedding an object, and you would be right. However, there is an important difference in how the data is stored on MongoDB and how we used it. While embedding, the whole object or an array of whole objects is saved inside the other, and when referencing, only the `id` attribute of the objects is saved—referencing is like a one-to-many relationship.

The next step is to understand how to use referenced objects. Let's take a look at the `Client` snippet. If you take a look at the `prepareClients()` method, you'll see that it creates a client, sets the name, and invokes the `saveTheRecord()` method, which returns a value of the type `Box[Client]`. It then invokes the `map` method and then the `prepareOrders` method, passing the boxes' value as the first argument and a decimal number as the second argument. Then, the `prepareOrders` method creates a new order, sets it into the client's `orders` object, and saves the client. These steps are repeated two more times to create three orders and three clients.

After creating the clients and the orders, the `list` method invokes the `findAll` method from the `Client` object to fetch all clients from MongoDB. Then for each client, it invokes the `objs` method from the client's `orders` object; this then fetches the list of referenced objects and caches them. Once it gets the list of orders referenced by the `client` object, it iterates the list and creates a string with the date and the total value of the order to be rendered on the web page.

See also...

▶ You can navigate to the following URL to learn more about referenced objects:

`https://www.assembla.com/wiki/show/liftweb/Mongo_Record_Referenced_Objects`

Querying with Rogue

Rogue is a type-safe **domain specific language** (**DSL**) built by Foursquare to execute, find, and modify commands against MongoDB using Lift. You can use Rogue to enhance the power of your `record` models.

In this recipe, we will learn the basics of Rogue to perform a couple of queries using its features.

Getting ready

We'll evolve the project from the *Mapping a MongoDB collection to a Scala class* recipe but you'll need to add Rogue in the list of dependencies of the project. Add the following lines in the `libraryDependencies` `Seq` key in the `build.sbt` file:

```
    "com.foursquare"    %% "rogue-field"    % "2.2.0"
intransitive(),
    "com.foursquare"    %% "rogue-core"     % "2.2.0"
intransitive(),
    "com.foursquare"    %% "rogue-lift"     % "2.2.0"
intransitive(),
    "com.foursquare"    %% "rogue-index"    % "2.2.0"
intransitive()
```

How to do it...

Carry out the following steps:

1. Add the following `import` statements in the `Client.scala` file:

   ```
   import com.foursquare.rogue.LiftRogue._
   import java.util.regex.Pattern
   ```

2. Modify the `Client` class companion object as follows:

   ```
   object Contact extends Contact with MongoMetaRecord[Contact] {
     def startsWith(name: String) = {
       val pattern = Pattern.compile(name + ".*", Pattern.CASE_
   INSENSITIVE | Pattern.MULTILINE)

       Contact where (_.name matches pattern) fetch()
     }

     def fetchWithLimit(limit: Int) = Contact.orderAsc(_.name).
   fetch(limit)

     def findByName(name: String) = Contact.where(_.name eqs name).
   get()
   }
   ```

3. In the `Clients.scala` file, add two more names in the `contactsName` list:

   ```
   val contactsNames = "John" :: "Joe" :: "Lisa" :: "Bill" ::
   "Brandon" :: Nil
   ```

4. Replace the `list` method with the following code:

```
def list = {
  prepareContacts_!()
  ".starts-with li *" #> Contact.startsWith("B").map(_.name.get)
  &
  ".first-three li *" #> Contact.fetchWithLimit(3).map(_.name.
get) &
  ".get-by-name *" #> Contact.findByName("Lisa").map(_.name.
get).getOrElse("")
}
```

5. In the `index.html` file, replace the HTML code inside the `div` tag with `id` set to `main` with the following HTML snippet:

```
<div data-lift="Contacts.list">
  <h6>Found by name: <span class="get-by-name"></span></h6>

  <h6>Starts with 'B'</h6>
  <ul class="starts-with">
    <li></li>
  </ul>

  <h6>First 3 contacts</h6>
  <ul class="first-three">
    <li></li>
  </ul>
</div>
```

6. Start the application.

7. Access `http://localhost:8080` and you'll see a web page like the one in the following screenshot:

How it works...

As you can see, there is nothing new regarding the `Contacts` code snippet and the `index.html` file. In the snippet, we just added two more names into the list, and then we changed the code from the `list` method to use the new methods we added into the `Contact` object. Let's see what each one of them does. The `findByName` method takes one string as argument—the contact name—and then invokes the `where` method from the `Contact` companion object. But wait! `MetaRecord` objects don't have a `where` method, so how did we use such method?

As it turns out, Rogue comes with several implicit conversion methods to better integrate with `record`. One of the implicit conversions is from `MetaRecord` to `QueryBuilder`. So, as you can imagine, when we used `Contact.where`, we weren't invoking it from the `Contact` object but from Rogue's `QueryBuilder` object. The `where` methods take the clause we want to add in the query as an argument and returns a `Query` object.

When we used this `_.name eqs name` as the query clause, we told Rogue to get only the contacts whose `name` field is equal to the value of the variable `name`. The `eqs` method you see in the `where` clause takes a value as an argument and compares it with the value of the field.

The `startsWith` method is similar to `findByName`, but is used instead of the `eqs` method to find contacts whose name matches exactly with the argument passed to the method.

We built a `Pattern` object, a compiled representation of a regular expression—to match the strings that start with the value—that was used to invoke the `startsWith` method. Finally, we passed the `Pattern` object to the `matches` method, which will be used to find the contacts whose names match the pattern.

Then, we invoked the `fetch` method from the `Query` object to return all records that were found. In the `fetchWithLimit` method, we used two methods from Rogue. The first is `orderAsc`, and the second is `fetch`. The same implicit conversion that was applied to convert a `MetaRecord` object into a `QueryBuilder` object (so we could use the `where` method) was applied here. That's why we used the `orderAsc` method without any problems. As you can imagine, the `orderAsc` method orders the result of the query in an ascending order, using the value of the field that was passed as its parameter to sort the result, in our case, the names of the contacts. The `fetch` method in the `fetchWithLimit` and `startsWith` methods are not the same. In the latter, it just executes the query, while in the former, it implicitly adds a limit clause to the query before executing it.

To explicitly limit the number of records that a query might return, you should use this code:

```
Contact.orderAsc(_.name)..limit(3).fetch()
```

Here, 3 specifies the maximum number of records that the query will return.

See also...

▸ You can learn more about Rogue by visiting `https://github.com/foursquare/rogue`

▸ To learn more about regular expressions in Java, go to `docs.oracle.com/javase/tutorial/essential/regex/`

8
Integrating Lift with Social Media

In this chapter, we will learn:

- ▸ Signing up using a Facebook account
- ▸ Fetching a user's Facebook data
- ▸ Signing up using a Gmail account
- ▸ Fetching a user's Gmail data
- ▸ Signing up using a LinkedIn account
- ▸ Fetching a user's LinkedIn data
- ▸ Signing up using a Twitter account
- ▸ Fetching a user's Twitter data

Introduction

Social media is an important part of our daily lives, so much so that we use our accounts not only for interaction with our friends or colleagues, but also to log in on several online services and then share information from the social media account with the service you signed up for. This is called **social login**, and the **OAuth protocol** is used to authenticate the user and to obtain access the user's data.

There are two versions of the OAuth protocol. The first version is referred to as **OAuth**, while the second one is known as **OAuth2**. The version that will be used to share information will depend on the third-party application you are integrating with. For example, Facebook provides an API that uses OAuth2 but Twitter does not. So you can use OAuth2 to integrate your application with Facebook; but to integrate with Twitter, you need to use OAuth.

In this chapter, we will learn how to build such interaction between social media such as Facebook and Twitter with an application built using Lift.

Signing up using a Facebook account

In this recipe, we will see how to log a user in to your application using his/her Facebook account.

Getting ready

Before being able to integrate our application with Facebook, we need to register an application on Facebook. This will give us an application identification and a secret token that will be used to identify the application requesting authorization and access to the user's data.

1. Start a new blank project.

2. Edit the `build.sbt` file by adding the following dependencies:

   ```
   "net.databinder.dispatch" %% "dispatch-core" %
   "0.11.0",     "com.restfb" % "restfb" % "1.6.12"
   ```

3. Create a new app on Facebook and add its `id` and `secret` keys in the `default.props` file:

   ```
   facebook.app.id=<app-id>
   facebook.app.secret=<app-secret>
   ```

> To learn how to register an application on Facebook, please navigate to this URL: `https://developers.facebook.com/docs/web/tutorials/scrumptious/register-facebook-application/`.

How to do it...

Carry out the following steps to sign a user up using a Facebook account:

1. Create a file called `FacebookDispatcher.scala` inside the `code.lib` package:

   ```
   package code.lib

   import net.liftweb.http._
   import net.liftweb.http.{Req => LiftReq}
   import net.liftweb.common.{Loggable, Box, Full, Empty}
   import net.liftweb.util.Props
   import dispatch._
   import scala.concurrent.ExecutionContext.Implicits.global
   import net.liftweb.util.Helpers._

   object facebookSession extends SessionVar[Box[String]](Empty)
   ```

```scala
object FacebookDispatcher extends Loggable {
  val facebookAppId = Props.get("facebook.app.id").get
  val facebookAppSecret = Props.get("facebook.app.secret").get

  def signup(): Box[LiftResponse] = {
    val fbUrl = :/("www.facebook.com").secure / "dialog" / "oauth" <<?
      ("client_id", facebookAppId) ::
        ("redirect_uri", "http://localhost:8080/fb/callback") ::
Nil

    Full(RedirectResponse(fbUrl.url))
  }


  private def extractTokenFromString(strResponse: String) = {
    strResponse.split("&").map { param =>
      val keyValue = param.split("=")
      keyValue(0) -> keyValue(1)
    }.toMap[String, String]
  }

  private def processResponse(response: Future[String]) {
    val futureToken = for { strResponse <- response } yield {
      val paramMap = extractTokenFromString(strResponse)
      paramMap.get("access_token")
    }

    facebookSession(futureToken())
  }

  def callback(): Box[LiftResponse] = {

    val redirectUrl = "http://localhost:8080/fb/callback"

    S.param("code") match {
      case Full(c) => {
        val reqHandler = :/("graph.facebook.com").secure / "oauth" / "access_token" <<?
          ("client_id", facebookAppId) ::
            ("redirect_uri", redirectUrl) ::
            ("client_secret", facebookAppSecret) ::
            ("code", c) :: Nil
```

```
            val resp = Http(reqHandler OK as.String)

            processResponse(resp)
          }
          case _ => logger.warn("no code parameter in the URL")
        }

        Full(RedirectResponse("/"))
      }

      def matcher: LiftRules.DispatchPF = {
        case req @ LiftReq("fb" :: "login" :: Nil, _, GetRequest) =>
          () => signup()
        case req @ LiftReq("fb" :: "callback" :: Nil, _, GetRequest)
  =>
          () => callback()
      }
    }
```

2. Create a snippet called `FacebookData`:

```
package code.snippet

import code.lib.facebookSession
import com.restfb.DefaultFacebookClient
import com.restfb.types.User
import net.liftweb.util.BindHelpers._
import net.liftweb.common.Full

class FacebookData {
  def render = {
    facebookSession.get match {
      case Full(token) =>
      val facebookClient = new DefaultFacebookClient(token)
      val fbUser = facebookClient.fetchObject("me", classOf[User])

      ".id" #> fbUser.getId &
      ".name" #> fbUser.getName &
        ".email" #> fbUser.getEmail
      case _ => "*" #> "Not authorized"
      }
    }
  }
```

3. Append the `FacebookDispatcher` object into the `LiftRules.dispatch` value:

```
LiftRules.dispatch.append(FacebookDispatcher.matcher)
```

4. Replace the contents of the `div` tag with `main` as the value of `id` in the `index.html` file with the following HTML code:

```html
<head_merge>
        <style type="text/css">
            button {
                display: block;
                margin-bottom: 40px;
            }
        </style>
    </head_merge>

    <h2>Welcome to your project!</h2>

    <a href="http://localhost:8080/fb/login">Log in using
Facebook</a>
        <div data-lift=" FacebookData.render">
            <h3>Facebook User</h3>

            <dl>
                <dt>Id</dt>
                <dd><span class="id"></span></dd>
                <dt>Name</dt>
                <dd><span class="name"></span></dd>
                <dt>E-mail</dt>
                <dd><span class="email"></span></dd>
            </dl>
        </div>
```

5. Start the application.

6. Access `http://localhost:8080`.

7. Click on the **Log in using Facebook** link, and you'll be redirected to Facebook's authorization page, and when Facebook redirects you to the application, you'll see a web page containing your Facebook data, as shown in the following screenshot:

How it works...

Facebook's login mechanism uses OAuth2—a two-step authorization process. In the first step, we get a code which we can use to get an access token; only after getting the token will we be able get the user's data. With this in mind, to create the login mechanism to our application using the user's Facebook account, we'll need to get the code, take the access token, and then get the user's data so that we can store it in our database to be able to identify the user later.

When the user clicks on the link, we redirect him/her to the /fb/login URI, which is handled by the FacebookDispatcher object. If you take a look at the FacebookDispatcher .matcher method, you will see that the /fb/login URI invokes the signup method. The signup method redirects the user to Facebook so that he/she can authorize our application to get his/her data. Let's take a look at how it creates the URL to redirect the user.

We need to pass at least the following two parameters to Facebook in order to get an authorization token:

- ▶ client_id: This is the app ID we set in the default.props file
- ▶ redirect_uri: This is the address that the user will be redirected to after Facebook's authorization process

To build the URL, we used the dispatch library, which is a library for interacting with HTTP in an asynchronous way. The :/ object creates a request to a host (www.facebook.com) which is the parameter passed to the method. Note that we didn't define the request's protocol, that is, if it's HTTP or HTTPS. That's why we invoked the method secure—which converts the request into a secure one—so that the request will be made to https://www.facebook.com.

After building the basics—host and protocol—of the request, we still need to define the path, which is done by using the method `/`. This method returns a new `Req` object, which is the result of combining the original `Req` object to the string that is passed as its argument. So, when we used `/` `"dialog"` `/` `"oauth"`, we created a request to `http://www.facebook.com/dialog/auth`. Then, we invoked the method `<<?` to add query parameters into the `Request` class. This method takes a list of tuples as parameter, where each tuple is composed of two strings— `(String, String)`. The first element of the tuple is the **query string parameter**, while the second of is the value.

You can see that we are adding two parameters into the `Request` class: `("client_id", facebookAppId)`, and `("redirect_uri", "http://localhost:8080/fb/callback")`. The first is the app ID and the second is the redirect URI which will send the user back to our application at `/fb/callback`.

Finally, we transform the `Request` class built by the dispatch library into an URI and then into a string. This is so we can pass it to the `RedirectResponse` object to finally redirect the user to Facebook.

You can see that we used the dispatch library just to build the correct HTTP request, and that issuing the `RedirectReponse` will make the user's web browser actually perform it; then Facebook will check whether the user is logged in or not. If not, it will display a login form, and once the user is logged in into his/her Facebook account, a form asking for the user's authorization will be displayed. Once the user authorizes our application to fetch data on their behalf, Facebook will redirect the user back to us, using the URI passed with the `redirect_uri` parameter.

The `/fb/callback` URI is also handled by the `FacebookDispatcher` object, which will invoke the `callback` method. The `callback` parameter method first checks if there is a query string parameter called `code` ("an encrypted string unique to each request", as per the Facebook developer site: `https://developers.facebook.com/docs/facebook-login/login-flow-for-web-no-jssdk/`), which is the signal that everything is ok and the user is authorized in our application.

 To make things simple, we are not handling any error case which would have resulted in the callback from Facebook not containing the `code` parameter.

Once we get the code, we will need to make another request to Facebook in order to get the access token. This request will be made to `https://graph.facebook.com/oauth/access_token`, and it will have the following parameters:

- `client_id`: This parameter is the app ID
- `redirect_uri`: This parameter is the address that the user will be redirected to after Facebook's authorization process

- ► `client_secret`: This parameter is the client secret that we added into the `default.props` file
- ► `code`: This parameter is the code that we've just got from Facebook

The difference here is that instead of making the request from the user's web browser, we've made it from the server. We did this by invoking the `Http` object, which is an **HTTP executor**. This means that it takes a request handler object and returns a `Future[Response]` object. However, instead of just passing the request handler, we have used some useful features of the dispatch library to make the `Http` object return a `Future[String]` object, where the `Future` will give us the data Facebook sent us.

Note that we passed the code `reqHandler OK as.String` as an argument to the `Http` object; `reqHandler` is the `Req` object. The `OK` method takes a function as its argument and executes the function only if the response returns a status code `200`; otherwise, it throws an exception. The function we are passing to the `OK` method is the `as.String` object. This object takes a response and returns its body as a string. In other words, `val resp = Http(reqHandler OK as.String)` will assign a `Future[String]` object to the `resp` value.

The problem is that a `Future` object is only a promise that says that, at some point in the future, we'll get something back from it. To get the value from `Future`, we invoked the `processResponse` method, passing `Future[String]` to it. This method uses Scala's `for` comprehension to get the string sent by Facebook and then invokes the `extractTokenFromString` method. Then, it will return a map containing all parameters sent with the response, which will allow us to get the value of the `access_token` parameter from it.

The `for` comprehension will return an object of type `Future[Option[String]]`, which still represents only a promise, and will assign it as the value of `futureToken`. So, in order to get the access token and use it, we need to evaluate `Future` to get the `Option[String]` object. We do this in the same way we were invoking a method called `futureToken()`. By doing this, we are applying the `Future` object and allowing it to be evaluated.

At the end, we applied the result of evaluating `Future` to the `facebookSession` object and we then redirected the user to the index page—`Full(RedirectResponse("/"))`. Now, if you take a look at the `FacebookData` snippet. you'll see that it checks whether the `facebookSession` object is full or not. If isn't, it will render a `Not authorized` string, and if it's full, it will use the `restfb` library to get the user's data and show it. In order to use `restfb`, we need to build a client using the access token `val facebookClient = new DefaultFacebookClient(token)`.

Then, having built the client, we invoked the `fetchObject` method by passing the string `me` and the class of the `User` object—`classOf[User]`—which will allow `restfb` to give us an instance of the `User` object populated with the Facebook public profile data. Then we can get the information from the `User` object and render it on the page.

There's more...

We stopped the process just after getting the user's information from Facebook and rendered it to make the example as simple as possible. To finish the login process, it would be necessary to save the access token and the information we got and put it into the database so that we could use it later without having to ask the user to repeat the whole process. So, what we would do is:

1. Ask for the user's Facebook e-mail ID using the access token.
2. Check if the e-mail ID exists in the database:
   - ❏ If it exists, store the user information in a `SessionVar` object
   - ❏ If it does not exist, save it and store the information in `SessionVar`
3. Use the information in `SessionVar` to acknowledge that the user is logged in.

See also...

▸ To learn more about the OAuth protocol, visit `http://oauth.net/`

▸ You can learn more about the Facebook API in Facebook's developer area:

`https://developers.facebook.com/`

▸ You can learn more about the `restfb` library at `http://restfb.com/` and about the dispatch library at `http://dispatch.databinder.net/Dispatch.html`

▸ If you have doubts about the database process, you can check *Chapter 5*, *Working with Databases* and *Chapter 6*, *Working with Record*.

Fetching a user's Facebook data

In the previous recipe, we learned how to log a user in using his/her Facebook account. Now, we will learn how to download more information about the user from Facebook, such as the user's friends.

Getting ready

You can modify the previous recipe's project or duplicate it so that you can keep both versions at hand.

How to do it...

A user's Facebook data can be fetched by carrying out the following steps:

1. Modify the `signup` method on the `FacebookDispatcher` object as follows:

```
def signup(): Box[LiftResponse] = {
  val scope = ("email" :: "friends_about_me" ::
Nil).mkString(",")
  val fbUrl = :/("www.facebook.com").secure / "dialog" /
"oauth" <<?
    ("client_id", facebookAppId) ::
      ("redirect_uri",
"http://localhost:8080/fb/callback") ::
        ("scope", scope) ::
        Nil

  Full(RedirectResponse(fbUrl.url))
}
```

2. Modify the `FacebookData` snippet to look like this:

```
package code.snippet

import com.restfb.{Parameter, DefaultFacebookClient}
import com.restfb.types.User
import scala.collection.JavaConversions._
import code.lib.fbSess
import net.liftweb.common.Full
import net.liftweb.util.BindHelpers._

case class FacebookFriend(id: String, firstName: String,
lastName: String, userName: String)

class FacebookData {
  val fields = "id" :: "last_name" :: "first_name" ::
"username" :: Nil


  private def fetchUserData(facebookClient:
DefaultFacebookClient) = {
    val myFriends = facebookClient.fetchConnection(
      "me/friends",
      classOf[User],
      Parameter.'with'("fields", fields.mkString(",")))
    )
```

```
    val friendsList = myFriends.iterator().toList.flatten

    friendsList.map { user =>
      FacebookFriend(user.getId, user.getFirstName,
user.getLastName, user.getUsername)
    }
  }
  def render = {

    fbSess.get match {
      case Full(token) =>
        val facebookClient = new DefaultFacebookClient(token)
        val fbUser = facebookClient.fetchObject("me",
classOf[User])

        ".id" #> fbUser.getId &
          ".name" #> fbUser.getName &
          ".email" #> fbUser.getEmail &
        "li *" #> fetchUserData(facebookClient).map(
facebookFriend => {
          ".id" #> facebookFriend.id &
          ".userName" #> facebookFriend.userName &
          ".firstName" #> facebookFriend.firstName &
          ".lastName" #> facebookFriend.lastName
        })
      case _ => "*" #> "Not authorized"
    }
  }
}
```

3. Start the application.

4. Modify the index.html file by appending the following code inside the div tag with the data-lift attribute:

```
      <hr/>

      <h4>Facebook Friends</h4>
      <ul>
          <li>
              <span class="bold">Id: </span><span class="id"></
span> /
              <span class="bold">User Name: </span><span
class="userName"></span> /
              <span class="bold">First Name: </span><span
class="firstName"></span> /
              <span class="bold">Last Name: </span><span
```

```
class="lastName"></span>
        </li>
    </ul>
```

5. Add the following code into the `style` tag:

```
li {
    list-style: none;
}

.bold {
    font-weight: bold;
}
```

6. Access `http://localhost:8080`.

7. Click on the **Log in using Facebook** link and perform the authorization process. Now, you will see a web page containing your data and a list with your Facebook friends as shown in the following screenshot:

How it works...

The only difference between the login and authorization process is the scope, using this we've now told Facebook that we also want to access to the user's e-mail address and the data about his/her friends. The bigger difference lies in the snippet code. You can see that after getting the user data, we invoked a method called `fetchUserData` and used its result to change the contents of a `li` tag.

This method invokes the `fetchConnection` method from the `restfb.DefaultFacebookClient` object, passing the following values as parameters:

- The first parameter is the string `me/friends`, which is the type of connection we want to fetch, in this case the user's friends

- The second parameter is the connection type, in this case, the `User` class since the user's Facebook friends are also Facebook users

- The last parameter—`Parameter.'with'("fields", fields.mkString(","))`—defines which fields from the user's friend's profile we want to fetch. In this case, they are: e-mail address, last name, first name, and username

> Facebook's request parameters are parameters that you can pass with the request to modify both the input and the output types.

We've then got an object of type `Connection[User]`, which we transformed into an `Iterator[List[User]]` object by invoking it's `iterator()` method. We then invoked the `toList` method to transform the `Iterator` object into a `List` object, which gives us a `List[List[User]]` object. However, the inner `List` object is not a Scala `List` object, but a `java.util.List` object. To convert the Java `List` object into a Scala `List` object—so that we can use the method from the Scala List API—we used the Scala object `scala.collection.JavaConversions._`.

Now that we have a `List[List[User]]` object where both lists are Scala objects, we can invoke the `flatten` method to get a list of users—`List[User]`. Then, we traverse the list of users—`List[User]`—and create a `FacebookFriend` object for each element of the `facebookFriends` list.

The `FacebookFriend` class is a `case` class that will be used to render the user information on the page. However, it could be a Mapper or a `Record` class that would store the information in the database. We've made it a `case` class to make the example simple. After getting the list of `FacebookFriend` objects back from the `fetchUserData` method, the snippet iterates it and creates a `CssSel` object that will create one `li` tag for each friend downloaded from Facebook.

See also...

- You can learn more about Facebook's request parameters at:

  https://developers.facebook.com/docs/reference/api/request-parameters/

- You can learn more about conversions between Java and Scala collections at:

  http://docs.scala-lang.org/overviews/collections/conversions-between-java-and-scala-collections.html

Signing up using a Gmail account

In this section, we are going to learn how to log a user into your application using his or her Gmail account.

Getting ready

1. Start a new blank project.

2. Register your app.

3. Edit the `build.sbt` file by adding the following dependencies:

   ```
   "net.databinder.dispatch" %% "dispatch-core" % "0.11.0"
   ```

4. Add the values of `client.id` and `client.secret` in the `default.props` file.

   ```
   google.client.id=app-id
   google.client.secret=app=secret
   ```

How to do it...

Carry out the following steps to create a login mechanism using Gmail:

1. Create a file called `GoogleDispatcher.scala` inside the `code.lib` package.

2. Create a `SessionVar` object called `googleSession`:

   ```
   object googleSession extends SessionVar[Box[String]](Empty)
   ```

3. Create a `SessionVar` object called `googleAuthState`:

   ```
   object googleAuthState extends
   SessionVar[Box[String]](Empty)
   ```

4. Create a `case` class called `AccessToken`:

   ```
   case class AccessToken(access_token: String, token_type:
   String, expires_in: Int, id_token: String)
   ```

5. Create a `case` class called `VerifiedEmail`:

   ```
   case class VerifiedEmail(id: String, email: String,
   verified_email: Boolean)
   ```

6. Create an object called `GoogleDispatcher` with the following code:

   ```
   import net.liftweb.http._
   import net.liftweb.http.{Req => LiftReq}
   import net.liftweb.common._
   import dispatch._
   ```

```
import net.liftweb.util.Props
import net.liftweb.json.JsonParser._
import net.liftweb.json.DefaultFormats
import java.util.UUID
import scala.concurrent.ExecutionContext.Implicits.global

object GoogleDispatcher extends Loggable {
  implicit def formats = DefaultFormats

  private def state =
    UUID.randomUUID.toString.replaceAll("-", "")

  def signup() = {
    googleAuthState(Full(state))

    val params = ("client_id",
      Props.get("google.client.id").openOr("")) ::
      ("response_type", "code") ::
      ("scope", "openid email") ::
      ("redirect_uri",
        "http://localhost:8080/google/callback") ::
      ("state", googleAuthState.get.openOr("")) :: Nil

    val googleUrl = :/("accounts.google.com").secure / "o"
      / "oauth2" / "auth" <<? params

    Full(RedirectResponse(googleUrl.url))
  }

  private def getToken(code: String) = {
    val params = ("code", code) ::
      ("client_id", Props.get("google.client.id").get) ::
      ("client_secret", Props.get("google.client.secret").get) ::
      ("redirect_uri",
        "http://localhost:8080/google/callback") ::
        ("grant_type", "authorization_code") :: Nil

    val baseReq = (:/("accounts.google.com").secure / "o" /
      "oauth2" / "token").POST
    val googleUrl = baseReq <:< Map("Content-Type" ->
      "application/x-www-form-urlencoded")<< params

    val futureResponseBody = Http(googleUrl OK as.String)

    val futureToken = for { strResponse <-
      futureResponseBody } yield {
      Full(parse(strResponse).extract[AccessToken]
        .access_token)
    }
```

```scala
      futureToken()
  }

  private def fetchUserInfo(token: String) = {
    val getUserEmail = :/("www.googleapis.com").secure /
      "oauth2" / "v1" / "userinfo" <<?
        ("access_token", token) :: Nil

    val futureResponseBody = Http(getUserEmail OK
      as.String)

    val futureEmail = for { strResponse <-
      futureResponseBody } yield {
      parse(strResponse).extract[VerifiedEmail] match {
        case VerifiedEmail(id, email, verified) =>
          Full(email)
        case _ => Empty
      }
    }

    futureEmail()
  }

  def callback() = {
    (S.param("state"), googleAuthState.get,
      S.param("code")) match {
      case (Full(rs), Full(os), Full(c)) if rs == os =>
        for {
          t <- getToken(c)
          email <- fetchUserInfo(t)
        } { googleSession(Full(email))  }
      case _ => logger.warn("no code parameter in the URL")
    }

    Full(RedirectResponse("/"))
  }

  def matcher: LiftRules.DispatchPF = {
    case req@LiftReq("google" :: "login" :: Nil, _, GetRequest) =>
      () => signup()
    case req@LiftReq("google" :: "callback" :: Nil, _, GetRequest)
=>
      () => callback()
  }
}
```

7. Append `GoogleDispatcher` to the `LiftRules.dispatch` value:

```
LiftRules.dispatch.append(GoogleDispatcher.matcher)
```

8. Create a snippet called `GoogleData` with the following code:

```
package code.snippet

import code.lib.googleSession
import net.liftweb.util.BindHelpers._
import net.liftweb.common.Full

object GmailData {
  def render = {
    googleSession.get match {
      case Full(email) => ".email" #> email
      case _ =>  "*" #> "Not authorized"
    }
  }
}
```

9. Replace the content of the `div` tag with `main` as the value of `id` with the following code:

```
<head_merge>
    <style type="text/css">
        a {
            display: block;
            margin-bottom: 40px;
        }
    </style>
</head_merge>

<h2>Welcome to your project!</h2>

<a href="http://localhost:8080/google/login">Log in using
GMail</a>
    <div data-lift="GmailData.render">
        <h3>Gmail User</h3>

        <dl>
            <dt>Email</dt>
            <dd><span class="email"></span></dd>
        </dl>
    </div>
```

10. Start the application.

11. Access `http://localhost:8080`.

When you click on the **Log in using GMail** link, you'll be redirected to Google's authorization page and then it redirects you back to the application, where you'll see a page containing your Gmail e-mail address, as shown in the following screenshot:

How it works...

The process is similar to that in the *Signing up using a Facebook account* recipe. So, when the user clicks on the link, he/she is redirected to `/google/login`. This URL is handled by the `GoogleDispatcher` object, which invokes the `signup` method when a request is made to that URL.

To make the login process work, we need to first get an authorization token from Google, and then we have to make another request to get the access token, which we will use to get the user's e-mail address. The first request to get the authorization code requires us to pass some parameters in order to get the token. They are:

- `state`: It is a unique string that we use as an anti-forgery token.
- `response_type`: This should be `"code"`.
- `scope`: This should be `"openid email"`.
- `redirect_uri`: This is the address that the user will get redirected to after the authorization process. This URL must be registered when you register the application.

The **state token** is a random string created by the `java.util.UUID` class in the `state` method and then stored in the `googleAuthState` session variable. After getting the state token, the `signup` method generates a list of tuples to hold the parameters necessary to make the request—`params` variable—and then it uses the dispatch library to create the request URL:

```
:/("accounts.google.com").secure / "o" / "oauth2" / "auth" <<?
```

The user is then redirected to Google to authorize our application to get his data. Once the application is authorized, Google redirects the user to the URL we've passed in the `redirect_uri` param—`http://localhost:8080/google/callback`—and it also adds some query string parameters that we'll use to finish the process. This URL is also handled by the `GoogleDispatcher` object, which invokes the `callback` method after requests has been made to the `/google/callback` URL.

The `callback` method does a pattern matching to get the values passed in the URL as query strings and also to get the value from the `googleAuthState` session variable:

```
(S.param("state"), googleAuthState.get, S.param("code")) match {
....
```

If the URL has the state and code parameters (sent by Google) and the session variable is properly set, the method compares the state parameter with the value we stored in the session earlier. If they don't match, it does nothing; but if they match, it continues the process.

Now that we have the authorization code which was sent to us in the `code` parameter, we can ask for the access token by invoking the `getToken` method. This method does a POST request to Google, passing:

- `client_id` and `client_secret` variables: We set these in the `default.props` file
- `redirect_uri`: The same as before
- `code`: The authorization code we got from the previous step
- `grant_type`: This parameter must be `"authorization_code"`.

It also sets the `Content-Type` header of the `Request` class to `application/x-www-form-urlencoded`. Then, it uses Scala's `for` comprehension to parse the response received from Google and extracts the access token. Since the response is a JSON string, we've used Lift's `JsonParser` object to transform the JSON string into an instance of the `case` class called `AccessToken`.

Now that we have the access token, we can finally ask for the user's e-mail ID by invoking the `fetchUserInfo` method. To get the user's e-mail ID, the `fetchUserInfo` method sends a GET request to Google using the dispatch library by passing the access token as a query string parameter. Then, the method gets the JSON sent by Google, parses it using Lift's `JsonParser` object, and creates an instance of the `case` class `VerifiedEmail`, which has the user's e-mail ID.

Finally, it gets the e-mail address, sets it into the `googleSession` session variable, and redirects the user to the home page—`http://localhost:8080`. You can see that the `GmailData` snippet will add the e-mail address inside the `span` tag with class `email` if the `googleSession` session variable has some value; if not, it will add the text `Not authorized`.

See also...

▸ We have explained the basics about the dispatch library in the first recipe, *Signing up using a Facebook account*. You can refer to it if you have any queries.

▸ You can learn more about Google's OAuth API at:

```
https://developers.google.com/accounts/docs/OAuth2Login?hl=ja
```

Fetching a user's Gmail data

In this recipe, we will go a step further and learn how to get a user's Gmail contact list using the Google Data API.

Getting ready

1. You can use the same project we have used in the last section, or you can create your own.

2. Edit the `build.sbt` file by adding the following dependencies:

```
"com.google.gdata" % "core" % "1.47.1-custom"
```

How to do it...

Carry out the following steps to fetch a user's Gmail data:

1. Append the following code into the `div` tag with the `data-lift` attribute:

```
<hr/>

<h4>Gmail Contacts</h4>
<ul>
    <li>
        <span class="bold">Full Name: </span><span
            class="fullName"></span>
    </li>
</ul>
```

2. Add the following case class into the `GoogleDispatcher.scala` file:

```
case class User(email: String, accessToken: AccessToken)
```

3. Modify the `googleSession` SessionVar object from `Box[String]` to `Box[User]`:

```
object googleSession extends SessionVar[Box[User]](Empty)
```

4. In the `getToken` method, remove the invocation to the `access_token` variable when parsing the response string from the old code—from the login recipe— `Full(parse(str).extract[AccessToken]).access_token` to `Full(parse(str).extract[AccessToken])`.

5. In the `signup` method, modify the `scope` tuple in the `params` variable:

```
("scope", "openid email https://www.google.com/m8/feeds")
```

6. In the `callback` method, modify the `for` comprehension as follows:

```
for {
  t <- getToken(c)
  email <- fetchUserInfo(t.access_token)
} { googleSess(Full(User(email, t))) }
```

7. Create a new method called `getService` in the `GoogleData` snippet:

```
private def getService(accessToken: AccessToken) = {
  val service = new ContactsService("liftcookbook")
  service.setHeader("Authorization", "Bearer " + accessToken.access_token)

  service
}
```

8. Create a new method called `fetchContacts` in the `GoogleData` snippet:

```
private def fetchContacts(accessToken: AccessToken) = {

  val feedUrl =  new URL("https://www.google.com/m8/feeds/contacts/default/full")

  val query = new Query(feedUrl)

  getService(accessToken).getFeed(query,
classOf[ContactFeed]).getEntries.asScala
}
```

9. In the `GoogleData` snippet, modify the `render` method as follows:

```
def render = {
  googleSession.get match {
    case Full(user) =>
      ".email" #> user.email &
      "li *" #> fetchContacts(user.accessToken).map(contact => {
        ".fullName" #> contact.getName.getFullName.getValue
      })
    case _ =>  "*" #> "Not authorized"
  }
}
```

10. You'll also need to add the following `import` statements:

```
import com.google.gdata.client.contacts.ContactsService
import com.google.gdata.client.Query
import java.net.URL
import com.google.gdata.data.contacts.ContactFeed
import code.lib.AccessToken
import collection.JavaConverters._
```

11. Start the application.

12. Access `http://localhost:8080`.

    After the login process, you will see not only your e-mail, but also a list of your Gmail contacts, as shown in the following screenshot:

How it works...

Since the process to log the user in and get the user's authorization is the same, I'll only explain the things we've changed, why they were necessary, and the process of fetching the user's contact list from Google.

The first thing to notice is that we've changed the `googleSession` object from `Box[String]` to `Box[User]`. We had to make such a change because, unlike the time when we were just logging the user in, we're now going to make new requests to Google in order to get more information about the user, and for each request we issue, the access token is required. So, we've created a `User` object to store both the e-mail address and token so that we can use them later.

Since were requesting more information, we also need to change the `scope` parameter when requesting the token. For this purpose, we've added the URL `https://www.google.com/m8/feeds`. If we didn't add this URL into the `scope` parameter, we wouldn't be able to get the list.

You can see that in the `callback` method, instead of just storing the e-mail, we are now storing a `User` object in the session variable. Besides the scope and the changes which we made to store more information in the session variable, the process to get the token is exactly the same as the one we saw in the previous recipe.

In the `GoogleData` snippet, we have added two new methods—`getService` and `fetchContacts`. The former method creates an instance of the class `ContactsService`, which we'll use to fetch the contact list.

 Google's client library has different service classes for different types of information that you might want to get—`CalendarService` for integration with Google Calendar, `DocsService` to integrate your application with Google Docs, and so on.

To create the service object and be able to use it, we need to set it's `Authorization` header with the access token we got earlier—`service.setHeader("Authorization", "Bearer " + accessToken.access_token)`. We can now ask for the contact list. In order to get the list, we need to use the service object to perform queries on a given URL. This is exactly what the `fetchContacts` method does. It creates a `URL` object using the URI that contains the contacts list—`https://www.google.com/m8/feeds/contacts/default/full`—and it creates a `Query` object passing the `URL` object to its constructor.

Now that we have the `Query` and `ContactsService` objects, we can ask for the contact list by invoking the `ContactsService getFeed` method, passing the `Query` object and the class of the feed—`classOf[ContactFeed]`—which will give us a `ContactFeed` object.

We can then invoke the `getEntries` method to get a list of `ContactEntry` objects, one for each contact existing in the user's contact list. However, this returns a `java.util.List` object, and to make our life easier, we've used the `asScala` method from the `JavaConverters` object in order to convert the Java `List` object into a Scala `List` object.

We now have the user's contact list and we can display it in the web page.

See also...

▶   You can learn more about the Google Data API at:

    `https://developers.google.com/gdata/`

Signing up using a LinkedIn account

In this recipe, we'll continue our journey through social media and we'll make the user of your application capable of authenticating it using their LinkedIn account.

The authentication process using someone's account is just like the process we learned when authenticating the user using his or her Gmail account. This means that we first need to get an authorization token and an access token before being able to get information about the user.

Getting ready

1. You can use the project from the *Signing up using a Gmail account* recipe or you can create your own project.

2. Register your application on LinkedIn.

3. Add app id and secret into the default.props file:

   ```
   linkedin.client.id=api-key
   linkedin.client.secret=api-secret
   ```

How to do it...

Carry out the following steps:

1. Create a file called LinkedinDispatcher.scala with the same content from the GoogleDispatcher.scala file.

2. Modify the case class called AccessToken by removing the id_token and token_type attributes.

3. Remove the case class called VerifiedEmail.

4. Modify the params variable in the getToken method to use the correct key when getting the client id and secret variables from the default.props file.

5. Set redirect_uri to:

   ```
   http://localhost:8080/linkedin/callback
   ```

6. Replace the value of baseReq with the following code:

   ```
   val baseReq = (:/("www.linkedin.com").secure / "uas" /
     "oauth2" / "accessToken").POST << paramsRemove the
     googleUrl value declaration.
   ```

7. Rename the variable passed as an argument to the Http constructor from googleUrl to baseReq:

   ```
   Http(baseReq OK as.String)
   ```

8. Change the method `fetchUserInfo` as follows:

```
private def fetchUserInfo(token: String) = {
   val getUserEmail = :/("api.linkedin.com").secure / "v1" /
"people" / "~" / "email-address" <<?
      ("oauth2_access_token", token) :: Nil

   val futureResponseBody = Http(getUserEmail OK as.String)

   val futureEmail = for { strResponse <- futureResponseBody }
yield {
      Full(XML.loadString(strResponse).text)
   }

   futureEmail()
}
```

9. Modify the `params` variable in the `signup` method to use the correct key when getting the `client.id` variable from the `default.props` file.

10. Change the scope of `param` from `"openid email"` to `"r_emailaddress"`

11. Rename the occurrences of the `googleAuthState` session variable to `linkedinAuthState`.

12. Change the `redirect_uri` param to `"http://localhost:8080/linkedin/callback"`.

13. Replace the `googleUrl` variable declaration with the following code:

```
val linkedinUrl = :/("www.linkedin.com").secure / "uas" /
"oauth2" / "authorization" <<? params
```

14. Rename the occurrences of the `googleUrl` variable to `linkedinUrl`.

15. In the `callback` and `matcher` methods, replace the occurrences of the word `google` with `linkedin`.

16. Rename `GoogleDispatcher` to `LinkedinDispatcher` in the `Boot.scala` class.

17. The `GmailData` snippet will be turned into the `LinkedinData` snippet.

18. Replace the occurrences of the word `google` with `linkedin`.

19. Replace all occurrences of `google` with `linkedin` in the `index.html` file.

20. Start the application and access `http://localhost:8080`.

After the authorization process, you will see a web page showing the e-mail address you use for your LinkedIn account, as shown in the following screenshot:

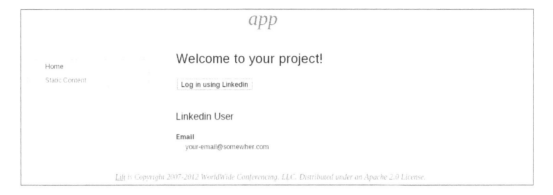

How it works...

The main point of re-using the code from the earlier recipe *Signing up using a Gmail account* was to show you that the process of signing users up using their Gmail or LinkedIn accounts is the same. That's because they both use OAuth2—Version 2 of the OAuth protocol.

This means that in both cases we need to make a request to get an authorization code. Then we need to make another call to get an access token which can be used on further requests to get the information we want about the user.

Besides the name differences, variable names, and so on, you can see that three things were actually different between both cases:

- The URL's we used to make the requests, for example:
  - https://accounts.google.com/o/oauth2/token
  - https://www.linkedin.com/uas/oauth2/accessToken
- When requesting the access token from Google, we needed to specify the request's Content-Type header, which wasn't necessary when requesting the token for LinkedIn
- While Google sends the data using JSON, LinkedIn uses XML, which means we need to change how we handle the responses we get from each one

▶ You can learn more about LinkedIn's REST API at:

```
http://developer.linkedin.com/rest
```

▶ If you are interested in learning more about the OAuth2 protocol, you can go to:

```
http://oauth.net/2/
```

Fetching a user's LinkedIn data

After learning how to sign users up to your application using their LinkedIn account, we will learn how to fetch the user's LinkedIn connection list.

Getting ready

We will modify the project we created in the previous section.

How to do it...

Carry out following steps:

1. Modify the `LinkedinDispatcher` object by changing the `scope` parameter in the `signup()` method from `"r_emailaddress"` to `"r_emailaddress,r_fullprofile,r_network"`.

2. Create a `case` class called `User` as follows:
   ```
   case class User(email: String, token: String)
   ```

3. Change the type of the session variable `linkedinSession` from `Box[String]` to `Box[User]`.

4. Change the `linkedinSess(Full(email))` code in the `callback` method to `linkedinSess(Full(User(email, t)))`.

5. Modify the `index.html` file by appending the following HTML code in the `div` tag with attribute `data-lift`:
   ```
   <h4>LinkedIn Contacts</h4>
   <ul>
       <li>
           <span class="bold">Full Name: </span><span
   class="fullName"></span>
       </li>
   </ul>
   ```

6. Modify the `LinkedinData` snippet by adding the following `import` statements:

```
import dispatch._
import scala.xml.XML
import scala.concurrent.ExecutionContext.Implicits.global
```

7. Create a `case` class called `LinkedinPerson`.

```
case class LinkedinPerson(firstName: String, lastName: String) {
   def fullName = firstName + " " + lastName
}
```

8. Create a method called `fetchConnections`.

```
    def fetchConnections(token: String) = {
      val params = ("oauth2_access_token", token) :: Nil
      val baseReq = :/("api.linkedin.com").secure / "v1" / "people"
/ "~" / "connections:(first-name,last-name)"
      val req = baseReq <<? params
      val futureResponse = Http(req OK as.String)
      val futureConnections = for (strResponse <- futureResponse)
   yield {
         (XML.loadString(strResponse) \  "person").map(p => {
            LinkedinPerson((p \ "first-name").text, (p \ "last-name").
   text)
         })
      }

      futureConnections()
   }
```

9. Modify the `render` method as follows:

```
    def render = {
      linkedinSession.get match {
        case Full(u) => ".email" #> u.email &
           "li *" #> fetchConnections(u.token).map(p => {
             ".fullName" #> p.fullName
           })
        case _  =>   "*" #> "Not authorized"
      }
    }
```

10. Start the application and access `http://localhost:8080`.

You should see a web page similar to the one shown in the following screenshot once the authorization process is complete:

How it works...

To fetch data from the user's LinkedIn account, we need to make some changes because we need the token to make the request get the data we want. In order to store the token and use it later in the application, we changed the `linkedinSession` session variable to store a `User` object which holds the user's e-mail address and access token, instead of just storing the user's e-mail address. Another necessary change was the scope when requesting the access token. When we wanted just the token to get the user's e-mail address to sign him/her in, we set the value of `scope` to `r_emailaddress`. But now, we'll ask for more information about the user, and that's why we've changed the value of `scope` to `r_emailaddress, r_fullprofile, r_network`. After making such changes, the application now stores the user's e-mail address and access token in the session variable which we will use to get the user's connections.

If you take a look at the `LinkedinData` snippet, you will see that we added a new method called `fetchConnections`. This method makes use of the dispatch library to issue a request to `https://api.linkedin.com/v1/people/~/connections:(first-name, last-name)?oauth2_access_token=<access-token>`, and then it parses the response from LinkedIn—XML containing all connections of the user—and transforms it into a list of `LinkedinPerson` objects, which belong to a `case` class we have created to hold the data we get from LinkedIn. Finally, the snippet uses the list returned by the `fetchConnection` method in the render method, which will cause the data to be displayed in the HTML.

You can see that whenever a social media uses the OAuth2 protocol to allow access to its API for third-party applications, the process of gaining access and then fetching data is basically the same.

Signing up using a Twitter account

We will now learn how to log users in to your application using their Twitter account. Unlike Gmail, Facebook, and LinkedIn, Twitter does not have an OAuth2 API where you can make requests on behalf of the user. This means that we can only use OAuth2 to communicate with a small part of their API.

Unfortunately, the API part involved in the process of verifying user credentials is only accessible via Twitter's OAuth API, which uses Version 1 of the OAuth protocol. I said unfortunately because more work—code, requests, and more—is necessary when working with OAuth. However, there is a neat library we can use to work with OAuth that will make our lives easier.

Getting ready

1. Start a new blank project.
2. Edit the `build.sbt` file by adding the following dependency:

   ```
   "org.scribe" % "scribe" % "1.3.5" % "compile"
   ```

3. Create a new app on Twitter and add its `id` and `secret` keys in the `default.props` file:

   ```
   twitter.consumer.key=<app-key>
   twitter.consumer.secret=<app-secret>
   ```

How to do it...

Carry out the following steps:

1. In the `index.html` file, change the contents of the `div` tag with `main` as the value of `id` as shown in the following code:

   ```
   <head_merge>
       <style type="text/css">
           a {
               display: block;
               margin-bottom: 40px;
           }
       </style>
   </head_merge>

   <h2>Welcome to your project!</h2>

   <a href="http://localhost:8080/twitter/login">Log in using
     Twitter</a>
   ```

```
<div data-lift="TwitterData.render">
    <h3>Twitter User</h3>

    <dl>
        <dt>Id</dt>
        <dd><span class="id"></span></dd>
        <dt>Name</dt>
        <dd><span class="name"></span></dd>
    </dl>
</div>
```

2. Create a file called `TwitterDispatcher.scala` in the `code.lib` package.

3. You will need the following `import` statements:

```
import net.liftweb.util.Props
import org.scribe.builder.ServiceBuilder
import org.scribe.builder.api.TwitterApi
import net.liftweb.http._
import net.liftweb.common._
import org.scribe.model.{Verb, OAuthRequest, Token, Verifier}
import net.liftweb.json.JsonParser._
import net.liftweb.json.DefaultFormats
```

4. In the recently created file, add a `case` class called `TwitterPerson`:

```
case class TwitterPerson(name: String, id: Int)
```

5. Also add an object called `requestTokenSess`:

```
object requestTokenSess extends
SessionVar[Box[Token]](Empty)
```

6. And another object called `twitterSession`:

```
object twitterSession extends
SessionVar[Box[TwitterPerson]](Empty)
```

7. Create an object called `TwitterDispatcher` with the following code:

```
object TwitterDispatcher {
  implicit val formats = DefaultFormats

  val clientKey = Props.get("twitter.consumer.key").get
  val clientSecret =
    Props.get("twitter.consumer.secret").get

  val service = new
    ServiceBuilder().provider(classOf[TwitterApi])
    .apiKey(clientKey)
    .apiSecret(clientSecret)
```

```scala
          .callback("http://localhost:8080/twitter/callback")
          .build()

    def signup = {
      val requestToken = service.getRequestToken
      val url = service.getAuthorizationUrl(requestToken)

      requestTokenSess(Full(requestToken))

      Full(RedirectResponse(url))
    }

    def callback(req: Req) = {
      for {
        oAuthVerifier <- S.param("oauth_verifier")
        requestToken <- requestTokenSess.get
      } yield {
        val verifier = new Verifier(oAuthVerifier)
        val accessToken =
          service.getAccessToken(requestToken, verifier)

        val request = new OAuthRequest(
          Verb.GET,
          "http://api.twitter.com/1.1/account/verify_credentials.
json
  ?skip_status=true"
        )

        service.signRequest(accessToken, request)

        val response = request.send()

        val twitterPerson =
          parse(response.getBody).extract[TwitterPerson]
        twitterSession(Full(twitterPerson))
      }

      Full(RedirectResponse("/"))
    }

    def matcher: LiftRules.DispatchPF = {
      case req@Req("twitter" :: "login" :: Nil, _,
        GetRequest) =>
        () => signup
      case req@Req("twitter" :: "callback" :: Nil, _,
        GetRequest) =>
        () => callback(req)
    }
  }
```

8. Append the `TwitterDispatcher.matcher` method to the `LiftRules.dispatch` `Seq` value by adding the following code into the `Boot.boot` method:

```
LiftRules.dispatch.append(TwitterDispatcher.matcher)
```

9. Create a snippet called `TwitterData` with the following code:

```
package code.snippet

import net.liftweb.common.Full
import code.lib.twitterSession
import net.liftweb.util.BindHelpers._

class TwitterData {
  def render = {
    twitterSession.get match {
      case Full(u) =>
        ".name" #> u.name &
          ".id" #> u.id
      case _ =>  "*" #> "Not authorized"
    }
  }
}
```

10. Start the application and access `http://localhost:8080`.

After the authorization process, you will see a web page containing your Twitter ID and name, as shown in the following screenshot:

How it works...

After clicking on the **Log in using Twitter** link, the user is redirected to /twitter/login, which is handled by the TwitterDispatcher object. The dispatcher will then invoke the signup() method. This method does a few things. It first uses the OAuthService object to get a request token, and then uses the token to get the authorization URL which will be used to allow the user to validate the request token. After getting the authorization URL, it stores the request token in the requestTokenSess session variable and redirects the user to the URL that it received in the previous step. This will redirect the user to Twitter to validate the request token. After the token is validated, Twitter will redirect the user to your application using the callback URL that was set during the creation of the OAuthService object.

The callback URL is also handled by the TwitterDispatcher object, which invokes the callback method. Then, it gets the verifier parameter that was sent by Twitter and uses it to create a Verifier object. Then, using the Verifier object and the request token we put into the session variable, it requests the access token by invoking the getAccessToken method from the OAuthService object. Now that we have the access token, we can make a signed request to Twitter and ask for the data we want.

To create the request, the callback method first creates an OAuthRequest object passing a verb and a string URL as the parameters to the OauthRequest object constructor. The verb is the request type—GET, PUT, POST, DELETE, and so on—and the URL is the address of the API endpoint.

In this case, we are going to make a GET request to http://api.twitter.com/1.1/account/verify_credentials.json?skip_status=true to get the user data, that is, the ID and e-mail address. Actually, this endpoint gives us more information. However, for this example, we are only interested in the user's ID and name.

After creating the request object, the method signRequest is invoked and the access token and the request object are passed as arguments. We can finally send the request to Twitter in order to get the information we want by invoking the send method from the OauthRequest object. When we invoke the send method, it returns a Response object. This object has a method called getBody, which we can call to get the string containing a JSON object that has the user data, sent from Twitter.

We then use Lift's JsonParser object method to transform the JSON string into an instance of the TwitterPerson object and set it into the twitterSession session variable. The last thing that is done by the callback method is to redirect the user to the home page.

When the TwitterData snippet starts to process the HTML after the redirection, it checks the twitterSession session variable, which now has the TwitterPerson object, and adds the username and ID into the HTML that will be displayed in the browser.

As you can see, OAuth requires more work than OAuth2. However, we can make our lives easier by using libraries such as Scribe that handle OAuth complexities for us.

▸ You can learn more about OAuth protocols at:

```
http://oauth.net/documentation/getting-started/
```

▸ Here is the link for the scribe library:

```
https://github.com/fernandezpablo85/scribe-java
```

Fetching a user's Twitter data

In this recipe, we will go a step further and learn how to fetch the user's data from their Twitter account. Since the process of authentication is the same as in the previous section, we will focus on the things we need to do to change the project we created in the previous recipe in order to get the information we want from the user's account.

Getting ready

You can modify the project we created in the previous recipe or you can duplicate it.

How to do it...

Carry out the following steps to fetch the user's Twitter data:

1. Create a new file named TwitterHelper.scala with the following code:

```scala
package code.lib

import net.liftweb.util.Props
import org.scribe.builder.ServiceBuilder
import org.scribe.builder.api.TwitterApi
import org.scribe.model._
import net.liftweb.json.JsonParser._
import net.liftweb.json.DefaultFormats

object TwitterHelper {
  implicit def formats = DefaultFormats

  val clientKey =
    Props.get("twitter.consumer.key").openOr("")
  val clientSecret =
    Props.get("twitter.consumer.secret").openOr("")
  val callbackURL =
    "http://localhost:8080/twitter/callback"
```

```scala
val service = new
  ServiceBuilder().provider(classOf[TwitterApi])
  .apiKey(clientKey)
  .apiSecret(clientSecret)
  .callback(callbackURL)
  .build()

def fetchTwitterPerson(requestToken: Token, accessToken:
  Token) = {
  val request = new OAuthRequest(
    Verb.GET,
    "http://api.twitter.com/1.1/account/verify_
      credentials.json        ?skip_status=true"
  )

  service.signRequest(accessToken, request)

  parse(request.send().getBody).extract[TwitterPerson]
}

def fetchUserFriends = {
  val request = new OAuthRequest(
    Verb.GET,
    "http://api.twitter.com/1.1/friends/list.json?
      skip_status=true"
  )

  val friends = for {
    token <- accessTokenSess
  } yield {
    service.signRequest(token, request)

    parse(request.send().getBody).extract[TwitterFriends]
      .users
  }

  friends.openOr(Nil)
  }
}
```

2. Create a case class called `TwitterFriends` in the `TwitterDispatcher.scala` file:

```
case class TwitterFriends(users: List[TwitterPerson])
```

3. Create an object called `accessTokenSess`:

```
object accessTokenSess extends SessionVar[Box[Token]](Empty)
```

4. Remove the following code from the `TwitterDispatcher` object:

```
    implicit val formats = DefaultFormats

    val clientKey = Props.get("twitter.consumer.key").openOr("")
    val clientSecret = Props.get("twitter.consumer.secret").
openOr("")

    val service = new ServiceBuilder().provider(classOf[TwitterApi])
      .apiKey(clientKey)
      .apiSecret(clientSecret)
      .callback("http://localhost:8080/twitter/callback")
      .build()
```

5. In the `signup` method, you'll need to change the `requestToken` and `url` variables as follows:

```
    val requestToken =
TwitterHelper.service.getRequestToken
    val url =
TwitterHelper.service.getAuthorizationUrl(requestToken)
```

6. In the `callback` method, you'll need to change the `accessToken` variable with the following code:

```
val accessToken =
TwitterHelper.service.getAccessToken(requestToken,
verifier)
```

7. Delete the following code from the `callback` method:

```
val request = new OAuthRequest(
        Verb.GET,
        "http://api.twitter.com/1.1/account/verify_credentials.
json?skip_status=true"
        )

    service.signRequest(accessToken, request)

    val response = request.send()

    val twitterPerson =
parse(response.getBody).extract[TwitterPerson]
```

8. Add the following code in place of the deleted code:

    ```
    val person = TwitterHelper.fetchTwitterPerson
    (requestToken, accessToken)

    twitterSess(Full(person))

    accessTokenSess(Full(accessToken))
    ```

9. Replace the `render` method in the `TwitterData` snippet with the following code:

    ```
    def render = {
        twitterSession.get match {
          case Full(u) =>
            ".name" #> u.name &
             ".id" #> u.id &
              "li *" #> TwitterHelper.fetchUserFriends.map(f => {
              ".idName" #> (f.id + " - " + f.name)
            })
            case _ =>   "*" #> "Not authorized"
          }
        }
    ```

10. Append the following HTML code after the `dl` tag in the `index.html` file:

    ```
    <hr/>

    <h4>Twitter Friends</h4>
    <ul>
        <li>
            <span class="bold">Friend: </span><span
    class="idName"></span>
        </li>
    </ul>
    ```

11. Start the application.

12. Access `http://localhost:8080`.

    After the authorization process, you will see a web page containing your Twitter ID, name, and a list of your friends, as shown in the following screenshot:

How it works...

In this example, we created the `TwitterHelper` object to keep things organized and simple for us to re-use the `OAuthService` object. Since OAuth makes us sign every request we want to make, it's easier if we keep the service object and the access token in a place where they can easily be re-used.

You can see that the `fetchTwitterPerson` method wraps all the processes involved in verifying the user credentials—this was discussed in the previous recipe. Wrapping the process of verifying the user credentials on a method made the `callback` method a little bit cleaner because now, we just need to invoke one method that gives us an instance of the `TwitterPerson` object, which will be put inside a session variable.

Another change we made to the `callback` method was to add the access token into a session variable so that we can re-use the access token that we put in the session variable in the requests we'll make in the future. If you compare the `fetchTwitterPerson` and `fetchUserFriends` methods, you'll see that they are quite similar. They both create an `OAuthRequest` object—only the URLs are different—and they both use the access token to sign the request before invoking the request's `send` method.

Another difference between those methods is the return type. The first one returns an instance of the `TwitterPerson` object, while the second method returns a list of `TwitterPerson` objects—each one representing one friend of the user.

Since we wrapped all the processes needed to fetch the user's list of friends, all we needed to do in the snippet was invoke the `fetchUserFriends` method and then iterate the list to create one `li` tag for each one of them.

This is all you need to do in order to display data for a given user in your application. You can also explore the Twitter API documentation in order to discover new endpoints that you can use to grab more information about the user.

Index

Symbols

_createTemplate method 140
_deleteTemplate method 140
_editTemplate method 140
_showAllTemplate method 140
_viewTemplate method 140

A

ajaxDeletePeople function 60, 61
Ajax form
   creating 71-77
API 89
application programming interface. *See* API
application tests
   in-memory database, using
      in 143-146, 174-177
asJson method 94
associate method 164

B

Blueprint CSS 7
Boot class 21
boot method 18, 91
BSON 179
BsonRecordField class 186

C

callback method 231
client
   server-side functions, invoking from 57-61
command2 variable 54
complex menu structures
   creating 35

configureMailer method 18
connection
   configuring, to database 120-123
ConsoleAppender 16
Contacts.prepareContacts_! method 130
container:start command 7
count method 142, 174
CourseStudents class 171
createClient function 102
createClient method 101, 111
createLine function 105
Create, Retrieve, Update, and Delete. *See*
      CRUD
CRUD 90
CRUD feature
   creating, CRUDify used 137-140
CRUDify
   used, for CRUD feature creating 137-140
CSS selector
   used, for HTML list creating 26-29
curPage method 142
custom error page
   creating 46-49

D

data
   creating, REST service used 97-102
   deleting, REST service used 105-108
   modifying, REST service used 102-105
   obtaining, from server 90-97
database
   connecting to, Squeryl used 148-151
   connection, configuring to 120, 121
   migrating, Liquibase used 157-159, 160

Thank you for buying
Lift Application Development Cookbook

About Packt Publishing

Packt, pronounced 'packed', published its first book "*Mastering phpMyAdmin for Effective MySQL Management*" in April 2004 and subsequently continued to specialize in publishing highly focused books on specific technologies and solutions.

Our books and publications share the experiences of your fellow IT professionals in adapting and customizing today's systems, applications, and frameworks. Our solution based books give you the knowledge and power to customize the software and technologies you're using to get the job done. Packt books are more specific and less general than the IT books you have seen in the past. Our unique business model allows us to bring you more focused information, giving you more of what you need to know, and less of what you don't.

Packt is a modern, yet unique publishing company, which focuses on producing quality, cutting-edge books for communities of developers, administrators, and newbies alike. For more information, please visit our website: www.packtpub.com.

About Packt Open Source

In 2010, Packt launched two new brands, Packt Open Source and Packt Enterprise, in order to continue its focus on specialization. This book is part of the Packt Open Source brand, home to books published on software built around Open Source licenses, and offering information to anybody from advanced developers to budding web designers. The Open Source brand also runs Packt's Open Source Royalty Scheme, by which Packt gives a royalty to each Open Source project about whose software a book is sold.

Writing for Packt

We welcome all inquiries from people who are interested in authoring. Book proposals should be sent to author@packtpub.com. If your book idea is still at an early stage and you would like to discuss it first before writing a formal book proposal, contact us; one of our commissioning editors will get in touch with you.

We're not just looking for published authors; if you have strong technical skills but no writing experience, our experienced editors can help you develop a writing career, or simply get some additional reward for your expertise.

Instant Lift Web Applications How-to

ISBN: 978-1-84951-978-6   Paperback: 96 pages

Get to know the Lift Web Framework quickly and efficiently using practical, hands-on recipes

1. Learn something new in an Instant! A short, fast, focused guide delivering immediate results

2. Develop your own Lift web applications, find practical examples for many common use cases

3. Learn how to build responsive web applications

4. Hands-on recipes with accompanying source code to help you get up to speed quickly

Instant Play Framework Starter

ISBN: 978-1-78216-290-2   Paperback: 70 pages

Build your web applications from the ground up with the Play Framework for Java and Scala

1. Learn something new in an Instant! A short, fast, focused guide delivering immediate results

2. Get started with Play 2.1

3. Build your own web application with Java and Scala

4. Handle user input with forms and access data with Ebean, Anorm, and Slick

Please check **www.PacktPub.com** for information on our titles

www.ingramcontent.com/pod-product-compliance
Lightning Source LLC
Chambersburg PA
CBHW080401060326
40689CB00019B/4097